WINGS OVER DARTMOOR

MILITARY AIRCRAFT CRASHES ON DARTMOOR 1939 - 1966

GRAHAM LEWIS

Wings Over Dartmoor
Military aircraft crashes on Dartmoor 1939 - 1966

Graham Lewis

First published in 2016 by Leesthorpes Publishing

Moorview, Davidstow, Camelford, North Cornwall, PL32 9YF
grahamddlewis@gmail.com

Copyright

ISBN 978-0-9955745-0-2

Layout design by Karl Triebel

Printed by Hedgerow Print Ltd., 16 Marsh Lane,
Lord's Meadow Industrial Estate, Crediton, Devon EX17 3ES

Back cover photograph: Tribute to US aircrew who died in Tigers Marsh crash 1943.

This book is dedicated to the
memory of my father Gerald Lewis who
waited years to see this book published.

Also to the memory of
servicemen of all nations
who died on Dartmoor.

We will remember them.

THE AUTHOR

Author Graham Lewis pictured with part of his display at the RAF Memorial Museum, Davidstow Moor, Cornwall

Graham Lewis is the leading authority on aircraft crashes in Devon and Cornwall and has spent nearly 30 years researching and investigating crash sites in the region. His vast collection of aircraft artefacts and photographs is displayed at the RAF Memorial Museum at Davidstow Moor, Cornwall, where it has drawn praise from guide book authors and visitors. He was instrumental in establishing a permanent memorial at Morchard Bishop, in mid Devon, to the crews of two Halifax bombers that crashed after colliding during a wartime night exercise, and a similar memorial at Manley Bridge on the Grand Western Canal, Tiverton, to the memory of the two-man crew of a Canberra jet bomber which crashed there in 1961.

Graham gives group talks and often loans artefacts to schools for history lessons, always making sure the school understands that the children should be allowed to handle the objects. He is a talented artist and some of his paintings appear in this book. Graham lives on the edge of a former wartime airfield in Cornwall, in the bungalow once occupied by the station commander.

The stories behind military aircraft crashes across Dartmoor from the beginning of the Second World War and the crews and rescuers involved

CONTENTS

ABIDE BY THE RULES

If you are going to use this book to visit some of the locations of wartime crashes you should be aware of certain rules and abide by them.

It is illegal to use a metal detector on Dartmoor and it is prohibited to dig at any historical site on the moor. Walk the moor and consider what it must have been like for the aircrew – many of them very young men – who flew over it in bad weather.

For walkers today, as with those wartime fliers, the rule is just the same – take care.

* Dartmoor's weather can change rapidly. Always ensure you are correctly clothed and equipped.

* Always carry a map and compass and know how to use them.

* Be careful not to disturb ruins and historic sites.

* Do not light fires.

* Leave gates and property as you find them.

* Protect plants and animals, take your litter home.

* Control your dog at all times. You should keep your dog on a short lead on areas of open country and common land between 1 March and 31 July to avoid worrying lambs and ewes and disturbing nesting birds. Also keep your dog on a lead during the lambing season between 1 December and 30 June on enclosed farmland.

INTRODUCTION

This is a hands-on, dirt under the fingernails investigation into aircraft crashes on Dartmoor between 1939 and 1966. I have spent almost 30 years searching among the archives and on the ground for information about air crashes in Devon and Cornwall, always with the aim in mind of eventually being able to provide a fitting and permanent reminder of those brave men who lost their lives in the two counties. I was finally able to do that in 2014 when my unique collection of aircraft artefacts was put on permanent display at the RAF Memorial Museum at Davidstow Moor in Cornwall, thanks to the generosity of the museum's founders, David Keast BEM and Marjorie Colwill.

This book, featuring most of the Dartmoor crashes is, I hope, the forerunner of other books about wartime air crashes in the region.

The incidents recorded here were not the only ones on Dartmoor. There were two in 1931. The first came in May of that year when Sir John Valentine Corden, the tank, car and aeroplane designer, had to force land his Tiger Moth near Crazy Well Pool because of fog.

The following month, it was the turn of Rudolph Messel, of Ford House, Drewsteignton, to have a lucky escape. He was the Labour candidate for South Molton and was on the campaign trail when the aircraft in which he was a passenger crashed into a hedge at Whiddon Down. He and the pilot were badly shaken but unhurt.

Rudolph Messel: crashed at Whiddon Down

Then in 1933, the pilot of another aircraft escaped injury when it came down in the corner of a grass field belonging to the Dartmoor Prison farm.

So aircraft incidents on Dartmoor were nothing new, but the war years, understandably, produced a considerable increase in crashes, especially after the United States Air Force moved into bases in the region. It is these wartime crashes that mainly concern us here.

Most of them occurred in the 365 square miles area that became the Dartmoor National Park (DNP) in 1951. Bad weather conditions were the most common factor. The towering tors and high hills were dangers enough for aircrews, but add valley fog and dense, clinging mist, perhaps a small navigation error, and you have a recipe for disaster.

When I began writing the book, I endeavoured to restrict myself to incidents which took place within the DNP boundary, but some were so close to it – such as the Fairey Fulmar crash at Yelland Farm west of Okehampton and the tailless Typhoon at Meavy - that I hope I will be forgiven for including them.

Another restriction I felt had to be made was including mostly those incidents in which the aircraft involved suffered category E damage – a write-off in civilian terms. I could have filled a book much larger than this one had I included every mishap from my records, but that, I decided, would bore the reader.

Allowing for all this, these pages contain the details of 74 crashes involving the deaths of 131 servicemen of many nationalities – 33 of those were crew of American bombers who were killed in four crashes in December 1943.

Many aircraft were returning from raids, damaged and heading for RAF Exeter, which was used as a landing strip for battle damaged aircraft. Navigation exercises often took aircraft over the moor with tragic results.

Even if crews were lucky enough to survive a crash, getting help involved making an arduous trek over difficult terrain, such as in the gallant rescue at Kitty Tor and the Christmas Day tragedy at Tiger's Marsh.

Not much remains now of the wartime crashes on the moor as the men of the 67 Maintenance Unit, based at Marshalsea's Garage at Taunton – now the site of Tesco – were experts in salvage and cleared more tonnage per month of aluminium than any other MU in the UK. Some of their clear-up operations were a story in themselves, such as their nine-day slog at Steeperton Tor, where tracked vehicles were used for the first time to clear up the wreckage of a PB4Y-1 Liberator, and the dangerous dig at Lee Moor for the remains of a Stirling bomber and its crew.

Sometimes local farmers were paid to perform the clean-up, such as George Mudge after the crash of a Lancaster on Standon Hill.

The only Dartmoor site containing much wreckage is that of another PB4Y-1 Liberator in the West Okement valley where an engine and large parts of airframe can still be seen. The many pits in the area were caused by souvenir hunters digging for the wreckage which had been buried there in the original clear-up operation by the Army.

Over the years, the DNP authority has had wreckage cleared from several sites, such as Tiger's Marsh and Flat Tor Pan, where a Sea Vixen crashed in 1965.

Many years ago, a local man told me that in the 1960s a party of workers from Devonport Dockyard were employed to clear up the remains of the West

Okement Liberator. They were dropped off and given directions, but on making their way over the moor they came across the B17 site at Tiger's Marsh instead and blew up and buried those remains before going home.

One wartime airfield came within the now DNP boundary and that was Harrowbeer, on the edge of the village of Yelverton, and several incidents involving aircraft from there are featured in this book. It was opened on 15 August 1941 and closed in 1945 when most of the buildings were knocked down and the land was returned to farmland. The blast pens, however, still survive.

Harrowbeer had some distinguished visitors, notably the President of the United States, Harry Truman, whose aircraft, named Sacred Cow, was diverted there from RAF St Mawgan. It was at Harrowbeer that legendary American fighter ace Don Blakeslee, of the 4th Fighter Group, crash landed his P51 after forgetting to lower his undercarriage.

Just outside the DNP boundary was Folly Gate airfield, near Okehampton. This was used by the Army Co-operation Unit which worked closely with the artillery at Okehampton Camp.

In all weathers and for many miles, I have trudged Dartmoor to locate and photograph the crash sites. Aviation archaeology has been a passion of mine since I was 11, when I was given my first piece of a crashed aeroplane, but I wish I had listened just a little more intently all those years ago when a man from my home town of Crediton, who had helped disarm some of the depth charges left after the crash of the submarine hunting Liberator above the West Okement valley, had spoken of this dangerous work.

The incidents featured here are told in chronological order and I have looked in greater detail at 34 of them. I also thought it worth including a little detail on RAF Sharpitor at Peek Hill, which played a vital role in the top secret Gee navigation aid, and RAF Hawks Tor near Shaugh Moor, an important link in the radar chain around the South West.

One final piece of information before I leave you in peace to read this book. Being a stickler for detail, I wanted to get the names of all those who died in air crashes on Dartmoor before producing this book, but in some instances I have had to admit failure.

My search for information, pictures and clues goes on. Perhaps some of my readers can help.

Graham Lewis, Moorview, Davidstow Moor, Cornwall PL32 9YF

Shielding his eyes from the sun, a fighter pilot scans the skies above Exeter hoping his missing colleagues will return. This sculpture, by Frances Margaret of Otterton, Devon, stands near the entrance to Exeter International Airport as a memorial to the men and women from many nations who served at RAF Exeter during the Second World War.

The South West Airfields Heritage Trust instigated the memorial as they wanted to ensure the historic integrity of the Exeter site was maintained. Twenty two fighter pilots, flying out of Exeter, lost their lives during the Battle of Britain.

The sculpture was inspired by an August 1940 mission during the Battle when 14 Hurricanes from Exeter were scrambled to confront more than 150 Luftwaffe fighters and bombers over Portland. Four aircraft and three pilots were lost.

STORY TITLES

RAF HAWKS TOR

The Chain Home radar system was used to detect incoming enemy aircraft and Hawks Tor, on the south west edge of the moor, was the site of a transmitter station which formed part of this system. It had two masts and the base of both of these can be seen today along with the ruins of many other buildings.

A wartime flight map of the area covered in this book

RAF SHARPITOR

On the western side of Dartmoor, Peek Hill became the home in 1942 of RAF Sharpitor, a master station in the south west chain for a top secret navigation system codenamed Gee. This was used to guide British bombers fitted with special receivers to targets deep into Europe, having a range of 400 miles at 10,000ft.

The main feature of the site was a 210ft (64m) wooden tower to which the aerials were fixed. Nissen huts to house the transmitter and a telephone exchange were erected and near the main road to Princetown a domestic site was built, again using Nissen huts, which included a guardroom, cookhouse and canteen, plus accommodation for 35 personnel, 12 of who were RAF ground radar-trained. The foundations of some of these structures can still be seen.

In the summer what a fine place to be posted, but in the winter it could be somewhat bleak!

The transmitter was upgraded in 1956 when the wooden tower was replaced by a steel one.

This is the steel mast which in 1956 replaced the original wooden one at RAF Sharpitor (Bill Wilkinson)

The blocked entrance to the Royal Observer Corps bunker on Peek Hill.

In 1970, Devon and Cornwall Police tried to take over the site and later Plymouth council wanted to use it as a training area for their juvenile offenders. Thankfully both schemes were rejected.

Just below the summit of Peek Hill, the Royal Observer Corps constructed an underground bunker - one of several on Dartmoor - to record nuclear bomb blasts and fallout should Britain have been attacked. The entrance and two air vents can still be seen, but the bunker has now been filled in.

DATE:	4 JULY 1939
LOCATION/AREA:	LOWER WHITE TOR, POSTBRIDGE
AIRCRAFT TYPE:	FAIREY BATTLE MK 1
SERIAL NO:	K9391
SQD/UNIT:	150 SQD / DG
BASE:	BENSON, OXFORD
TIME OF CRASH:	DAYTIME
CREW:	SGT PINSHER SGT J. DOLAN SGT J. COLTON
PURPOSE OF FLIGHT:	TEST FLIGHT
CAUSE OF CRASH:	FOG

NOTES:

The crew were lucky to escape. Had the Battle caught fire after its crash landing it might have been a different story. The crew followed a stream off the moor to find a farm.

George Stephens, of Powder Mills Farm, here wearing his Home Guard uniform, looked after the crew following the crash on Lower White Tor (Kenneth Day)

The Fairey Battle's crew (opposite) enjoy a cigarette after their lucky escape (Author's interpretation)

LOWER WHITE TOR BATTLE

It is an irony of war that an aircraft called Battle should be so hopeless at fighting. Pitched into battle against the invading Germans in 1939, the Fairey Battle was so outclassed by the German Me 109 that the 1,000 or so Battles in service with the RAF at the beginning of the war were withdrawn from frontline fighting at the end of 1940.

Aircraft Ministry cost-cutting in the pre-war years was the probable reason for the Battle being neither one thing nor the other; it pretended to be a bomber and a fighter but was neither.

It was, though, a good aircraft to train on which was why the three man crew of Fairey Battle K9391 set out from their 150 Squadron base at RAF Benson in good weather on 4 July 1939 for a training flight to Plymouth's Roborough airfield. Here they were to land and refuel before heading back to Oxfordshire. The pilot was a Sgt Pinsher, the wireless operator/navigator Sgt James Dolan and the air gunner, acting as observer, Sgt John Colton.

It should have been a straightforward flight, but as they neared their destination the mist rolled in and they were unsure of where they were.

Working out the flight duration, the crew reckoned they must be over Plymouth so Sgt Pinsher let the Battle descend slowly while dropping the undercarriage. Just as they broke through the mist, the ground loomed in front and they pancaked in on flat ground near Lower White Tor. The undercarriage snapped

and the Battle broke in two, but miraculously did not catch fire.

Sgt Pinsher's seat harness saved him from injury. Dolan and Colton had cuts and bruises to the head and one of them had dislocated a shoulder.

They had no idea where they were. The three men said later they puffed on cigarettes while deciding what to do. They then followed a stream off the hillside until they came across some campers near Powder Mills Farm, the home of George Stephens and his wife, Dorothy, and George's sister, Mabel.

Mabel said: "We first knew of the accident when some campers on the farm heard men shouting. With my brother they went in the direction of the shouts, found the airmen and brought them back to the farmhouse. When they crashed, they had no idea of their whereabouts and walked for over a mile and a half following a stream they had found.

"One of them was bleeding rather a lot from head wounds and another had a dislocated shoulder. The man with head injuries we laid down and made as comfortable as we could, to the others we gave tea."

The three airmen stayed with the family for around an hour until an ambulance arrived to take the two injured men to Tavistock Cottage Hospital. The pilot, Sgt Pinsher, remained until RAF personnel from Plymouth arrived.

A salvage team later removed the guns and instruments, but the wreckage was still there in June 1945 when the Dartmoor author Kenneth Day passed by. It may have been buried years later for in the 1960s, the RAF Museum came down with a team and excavated the remains. Despite my many inquiries, no one seems to know what became of them.

Powder Mills, where the Stephens family looked after the crew.

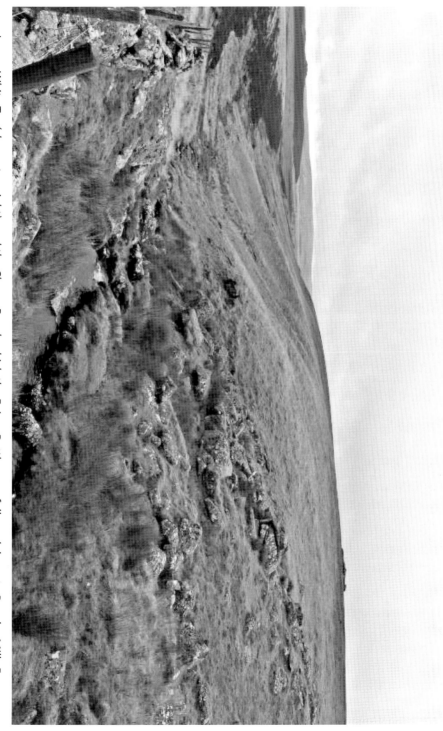

Lower White Tor (shown top right), and the Cherry Brook which the Fairey Battle crew followed down to Powder Mills Farm.

DATE:	18 JANUARY 1940
LOCATION/AREA:	YALLAND
AIRCRAFT TYPE:	AVRO ANSON MKI
SERIAL NO:	N5024
SQD/UNIT:	75 SQD / CODE AA / 6 GROUP
BASE:	HARWELL, NEAR SWINDON
TIME OF CRASH:	EARLY EVENING
CREW:	P/O BARRY STEVENS SGT FREDERICK SMITH SGT LESLIE CHENERY AC2 WILLIAM HERON AC2 LESLIE WAKELY
PURPOSE OF FLIGHT:	NAVIGATION EXERCISE
CAUSE OF CRASH:	SNOW STORM

NOTES: All the crew were killed when the Anson crashed near Shipley Bridge. The wreck was cleared by the RAF. This site is on private land.

WHITE-OUT

The night of 18 January 1940 saw heavy snow fall over Dartmoor. At Yalland Farm, near Shipley Bridge, the Hobbs family were sat around a blazing fire, the flames and light from the oil lamps giving the room a cosy glow.

For 12-year-old Sid and his brother, who were getting ready for bed, this was to be a night they would never forget.

In the skies above, 22 year-old pupil pilot P/O Barry Stevens was about to experience a pilot's nightmare and it would lead to the deaths of him and his four-man crew.

The Avro Anson, named after British admiral George Anson, had been built for a maritime reconnaissance role with a three-man crew, but it was not a success and its true role came to be training pilots for flying multi-engine bombers. The Anson was also used to train the other members of the bomber's crew such as navigators, wireless operators, bomb aimers and air gunners. It built such a strong reputation with the Operational Training Units that it became known affectionately as "Anson Annie". It was powered by two 350hp Armstrong Siddeley Cheetah engines, which gave few problems.

At RAF Harwell, near Swindon in Berkshire, the crew of Avro Anson N5024 took off for a Thursday night navigation exercise which would take them on a triangular course with Plymouth the turning point. P/O Stevens, who had graduated from Cranwell towards the end of 1939, was at the controls and was being instructed by veteran pilot Sgt Frederick Smith. With them were Sgt Leslie Chenery, 19, AC2 William Heron, 22, and AC2 Leslie Wakely, 19.

While flying over Plymouth the weather deteriorated quickly and they soon found themselves engulfed in a snow storm. P/O Stevens almost certainly suffered a white-out and could not see out of the cockpit. At this point, the Anson had just reached the slopes of southern Dartmoor.

Down below, the Hobbs family heard an aircraft flying low above them and then a loud bang. The house shook so much that the oil lamps blew out.

Young Sid's father put on his coat, lit a Tilley lamp and went outside into the snow storm. Just above the house he came across the tangled wreckage of the Anson in an area known as Yalland Marsh. The aircraft had not caught fire but all five crew had been killed. Mr Hobbs returned to the house to inform the authorities.

The police and RAF personnel arrived to remove the bodies and next day a reporter and photographer from the local newspaper turned up. Sid and his brother had their picture taken playing in the snow beside the shattered Anson.

Smith is buried at the Cathays Cemetery in Cardiff; Stevens, Wakely and Heron are buried side by side at the Harwell Cemetery in Berkshire and Chenery is buried in his home town, Chingford, Essex.

A white-out causes the fatal crash of the Avro Anson (Author's interpretation)

DATE:	16 MAY 1940
LOCATION/AREA:	MORETONHAMPSTEAD
AIRCRAFT TYPE:	BRISTOL BLENHEIM MK IV
SERIAL NO:	L9031
SQD/UNIT:	NO. 2 SCHOOL OF ARMY CO-OPERATION /CODE LX / 70 GROUP
BASE:	ANDOVER
TIME OF CRASH:	15.05HRS
CREW:	P/O MICHAEL PATTON-BETHUNE SGT KENNETH STOKES AC2 CHARLES CROWCROFT LAC HARRY MORTON
PURPOSE OF FLIGHT:	CROSS-COUNTRY, LOW FLYING EXERCISE
CAUSE OF CRASH:	FOG

NOTES:

This was the youngest crew to perish on Dartmoor.

A Blenheim Mark IV similar to the one which carried the youngest aircrew to perish on Dartmoor

YOU CAN TURN BACK

Army flying schools were issued with a new directive as a result of this crash of a Bristol Blenheim during a low flying exercise over Devon.

The MK4 Blenheim L9031 belonged to No. 2 School of Army Co-operation based at Andover in Hampshire and on 16 May 1940 its four-man crew were briefed for a low flying cross-country exercise which would take them across Devon to the turning point at Hartland, then to Plymouth before returning to Andover.

At the controls of the Blenheim was 21-year-old P/O Michael Patton-Bethune, a descendent of a French family of nobles. He came from Golders Green, London. With him was another pilot, 21-year-old Sgt Kenneth Stokes, of West Bridgford, Nottingham; the wireless operator/air gunner was AC2 Charles Crowcroft, 18, from Doncaster and the other crew member was LAC Harry Morton, 19, another Yorkshireman.

The flight went to plan until the Blenheim approached Dartmoor where the fog closed in. For P/O Patton-Bethune, who had only six hours on instruments, it would have been difficult to find a landmark on which to get a fix.

Just after 15.00hrs, the Blenheim crashed into the side of a hill close to the Moretonhampstead to Princetown road, killing all four crewmen. The site, being near the road, was cleared completely after the bodies had been removed. The deaths of Crowcroft and Morton, both RAF, were registered at Newton Abbot.

Stokes is buried at Hooe (St John) churchyard, Plymouth; Crowcroft at Doncaster Hyde Park; Morton at Halifax All Saints while the body of Patton-Bethune went to Golders Green Crematorium.

They were the youngest crew ever to be lost over Dartmoor.

After the tragedy, a directive went out to all flying schools suggesting dual flying for low flying flights and that schools should be conversant with the required skills for this type of exercise.

It also said that if in doubt about the weather, pilots should turn back. P/O Patton-Bethune would not have been blamed for turning back when the fog closed in.

ESCAPE TO VICTORY

Two Poles stole a French light bomber after the Battle of France had been lost and flew it to Devon.

The Breguet 693 they pinched was probably the most unusual of all the aircraft to crash on Dartmoor – and the locals thought the Poles were German.

The French air force, the Armee de l'air, received only 128 Bre 693s, which was powered by Gnome-Rhone 14M radials, and had a top speed of about 302mph. Mainly used for ground attack, it was no match for the anti-aircraft guns of the Germans and by June 1940 there were only 24 still flying.

The two Poles escaped to France – as many of their fellow fliers did – to continue the fight against Nazism from there, but when France fell these two determined and courageous men decided to escape to England.

Sometime after 12 June 1940, they stole the Bre 693 from an airfield in north-west France and flew across the Channel to England. They could have been attacked on the way because the bomber was full of bullet holes when it crash landed or perhaps it was like that when they took off and was the only one flyable after a Luftwaffe raid.

The two Poles flew over Torquay and Newton Abbot and, with fuel getting low, looked for somewhere to land. They flew low over Bovey Tracey, causing the locals to believe it was a German bomber, and picked out a field on the top of a ridge near the village of Hennock.

The aircraft touched down halfway into the field, which had been sown with barley, and slid for about 300yds before hitting a hedge.

The port engine hit the stump of an old ash tree and broke away from the fuselage.

Breguet 693 attack bomber

A Breguet 693, probably the most unusual aircraft to come down on the moor

The two Poles had come down at Bottor Rock Farm and were only slightly injured. They ran down the barley field shouting to a farm labourer who was pulling swedes in the next field, but he thought they were Germans and quickly made his escape to raise the alarm.

The Army soon arrived and the two Polish fliers were taken away for questioning and a guard was put on the crashed aircraft.

I was invited to visit the crash site in February 2003 by the farmer, Mr D.Harvey, who told me that at the time of the crash he was 13 years-old and away at school.

He said that after a day or so, the guard on the aircraft was taken away, but the aircraft remained on the site for some time and was a magnet for children from the farm and nearby village. Many parts were taken at this time.

During my visit, I found a few small parts of the aircraft near the hedge.

This is one of those unfinished stories. So far I have been unable to discover the names of the two Polish airmen or what became of them. Did they fly in the Battle of Britain? How did they manage to steal the Bre 693? Were they attacked during their cross Channel flight?

The search for information continues...

Mr D. Harvey stood by the impact point made in the hedge by the stolen aeroplane

DATE:	27 JULY 1940
LOCATION/AREA:	CHUDLEIGH
AIRCRAFT TYPE:	SUPERMARINE SPITFIRE MKI
SERIAL NO:	N3287
SQD/UNIT:	92 SQD
BASE:	PEMBURY, SOUTH WALES
TIME OF CRASH:	03.50HRS
CREW:	P/O TREVOR WADE
PURPOSE OF FLIGHT:	PATROL
CAUSE OF CRASH:	LOST, UNABLE TO FIND ANY LANDING GROUND

NOTES:

P/O Wade, known as 'Wimpy' after the hamburger-loving cartoon character in Popeye, fought in the Battle of Britain and won a DFC and AFC.

He was on patrol when his radio packed up and he became lost. He baled out safely. The abandoned Spitfire crashed south of Chudleigh. The crash site has since been built on.

After the war he was appointed chief test pilot at Hawkers. He tested the swept wing P1052 in May 1949, setting a new speed record for a London to Paris flight. He was killed while flying a P1081 on 3 April 1951 near Lewes, Sussex.

Test Pilot 'Wimpy' Wade postwar (anon)

High Willhays, the highest point on Dartmoor and in Southern England, where a Gloster Gladiator crashed.
(see following story)

DATE:	20 NOVEMBER 1940
LOCATION/AREA:	HIGH WILLHAYS
AIRCRAFT TYPE:	GLOSTER GLADIATOR
SERIAL NO:	N5644
SQ/UNIT:	247 SQD / CODE ZY
BASE:	ROBOROUGH, DEPARTED ST EVAL
TIME OF CRASH:	20.00HRS APPROX
CREW:	SGT ROBERT TUDOR THOMAS
PURPOSE OF FLIGHT:	SHIPPING PATROL OFF PLYMOUTH
CAUSE OF CRASH:	LOW CLOUD, OFF TRACK

NOTES:

Sgt Thomas, who had been lucky to escape a flying accident three months before, was posted missing after failing to return from his patrol. His body and the wreckage of his aircraft were found two days later at Dartmoor's highest point.

The last moments of N5644 over High Willhays (Author's interpretation)

CRASH ON ROOF OF DEVON

Walkers trudging over the roof of Devon could also be walking over the remains of an old biplane.

The burnt out remains of a Gloster Gladiator, which crashed at High Willhays killing its 22-year-old pilot, were cut up and buried there.

Nothing remains on the surface of this often squelchy highest point of Dartmoor (2,039ft) following the crash of Gladiator N5644 during a night patrol on 20 November 1940. Searchers looking for the missing aircraft had to be rescued themselves.

Roborough's grass airfield near Plymouth was home to the newly reformed 247 Squadron who had come from Shetland in July 1940 to defend the south west from enemy attack. They became operational in August and were one of only two squadrons to fly this biplane in the Battle of Britain.

The Gladiator was completely outclassed by enemy aircraft and reverted to a night defensive role, with some of Roborough's aircraft being based at St Eval in Cornwall.

The victory by the Few had already been achieved when Sgt Robert Thomas took off from St Eval at 20.00hrs in Gladiator N5644 for a Wednesday night patrol over Plymouth Sound and the coast.

How he ended up on Dartmoor is a mystery for when he failed to return it was not to the moors that his searchers went but out to sea.

The crew of Avro Anson R9071, of 217 Squadron based at St Eval, were looking for Sgt Thomas off Kelland Head between Port Quin and Port Isaac when their starboard engine cut out. P/O Holgate ditched the aircraft in the sea and he and Sgts Hickson, Taylor and Crowley had to be rescued by trawlers of the River Camel patrol.

Two days later, Sgt Thomas was found dead in the wreckage of his Gladiator at High Willhays.

It was the second time in three months that Sgt Thomas had been involved in a flying accident after getting lost. He was on a night patrol over Plymouth in Gladiator N5901 on Tuesday 27 August 1940 when he crashed into trees during a forced landing at Werrington near Launceston.

Sgt Thomas, who came from Battersea, London, is buried in St Stephen's churchyard, Bodfari, north Wales.

DATE:	24 NOVEMBER 1940
LOCATION/AREA:	HENNOCK, NR BOVEY TRACEY
AIRCRAFT TYPE:	WESTLAND LYSANDER
SERIAL NO:	T1530
SQD/UNIT:	225 SQD / CODE LX
BASE:	TILSHEAD
TIME OF CRASH:	16.15HRS
CREW:	P/O JUBB
PUIRPOSE OF FLIGHT:	ARMY CO-OPERATION
CAUSE OF CRASH:	BAD WEATHER

NOTES:

P/O Jubb was heading for Folly Gate airfield, near
Okehampton, when he became lost in bad weather. He force
landed in a field at Hennock, but because of the wet grass
the Lysander's brakes did not hold and he skidded into a
hedge. The aircraft was written off but the pilot escaped
injury.

*Westland Lysander: aircraft like this were used
on clandestine missions to Occupied Europe*

DATE:	29 DECEMBER 1940
LOCATION /AREA:	GREEN HILL
AIRCRAFT TYPE:	WESTLAND WHIRLWIND MKI
SERIAL NO:	P6975
SQD/UNIT:	263 SQD / CODE HE / 10 GROUP
BASE:	EXETER
TIME OF CRASH:	DAYTIME
CREW:	F/LT WYNFORD SMITH
PURPOSE OF FLIGHT:	ESCORT DUTY
CAUSE OF CRASH:	LOW CLOUD

NOTES:

F/Lt Smith was leading a section of three Whirlwinds to
Cornwall where they were to refuel before heading out to
escort two Catalinas inbound from Bermuda carrying VIPs.
The section became lost over Dartmoor and two of the
aircraft crashed. The wreckage and bodies were not found
until early March 1941.

The three Whirlwinds just before the crash with P/O Herbert
Kitchener's aircraft pulling up (Author's interpretation)

DATE:	29 DECEMBER 1940
LOCATION /AREA:	GREEN HILL
AIRCRAFT TYPE:	WESTLAND WHIRLWIND MKI
SERIAL NO:	P6978
SQD/UNIT:	263 SQD / CODE HE / 10 GROUP
BASE:	EXETER
TIME OF CRASH:	DAYTIME
CREW:	P/O DONALD VINE
PURPOSE OF FLIGHT:	ESCORT DUTY
CAUSE OF CRASH:	LOW CLOUD

NOTES:

P/O Vine was in a section of three Whirlwinds flying to St. Eval where they were to refuel before heading out to escort two Catalinas inbound from Bermuda carrying VIPs. The section became lost over Dartmoor and two of the aircraft crashed. Vine and Smith were believed to have collided.

Looking towards Green Hill where the two missing Whirlwinds were found

TOP SECRET LOSS

Sherlock Holmes author Sir Arthur Conan Doyle is said to have used Fox Tor mire on Dartmoor as the setting for the great Grimpen Mire in his most famous book, "The Hound of the Baskervilles".

There are many tales told about this most famous of the moor's miry places, but let me declare straightaway that the story about two top secret Westland Whirlwind fighters being buried in the bog is pure fiction.

Detailed research, like I carried out almost 20 years ago, would have proved to any would-be author and aviation enthusiast they were wasting their time hoping for a miry miracle.

The twin-engine Whirlwind, with four Hispano 20mm cannon in the nose giving it formidable firepower, was built at Yeovil in Somerset. It could have been a devastating attack aircraft had it been provided with Merlin engines and sufficient backing, but in the end only 114 of the type were made.

They were on the official secrets list until March 1941 and flying near Exeter and Dartmouth they caused air raid warnings to be sounded as they were not recognised by the Observer Corps.

On 29 December 1940, three Whirlwinds from Exeter-based 263 Squadron were ordered to fly to St Eval in Cornwall, where they would refuel, before flying out into the Atlantic to provide an escort for two Catalina flying boats inbound from Bermuda. These would have been US Navy Catalinas and were

The Westland Whirlwind could have been a world beater (Westland)

almost certainly carrying VIPs.

The section was led by F/Lt Wynford Smith, 25, from Worthing, Sussex, who had 42 hours on Whirlwinds with a total of 1,140 hours on all types. He was accompanied by P/O Donald Vine, 23, from Merstham, Surrey, with nine hours on Whirlwinds and a total of 305 on all types, and the experienced P/O Herbert Kitchener, 26.

Kitchener had been awarded a DFM in August, 1940 for his exploits with the squadron flying Gladiator biplanes in Norway. The King of Norway awarded him the Norwegian War Cross.

The three Whirlwinds took off that Sunday from Exeter at 12.05hrs. Kitchener flew on the starboard

Survivor: P/O Herbert Kitchener

side of Smith who carried the only map. Vine was on the port side of his leader.

The squadron's operational record book says that visibility was bad with 10/10 cloud at 200ft in places and the section became lost.

It goes on: "They came down to 300ft in the vicinity of Bovey Tracey, P/O Kitchener thinks. He reports seeing the ground immediately in front of him. He pulled up very quickly and thinks he saw a dull red flash on his right. Smith and Vine have not been heard of since."

Kitchener was ordered to return to Exeter, but was soon in the air again when he joined a six man flight in carrying out the escort mission. Meanwhile a search was made for the missing Whirlwinds, but nothing was found.

It was considered at the time that both Whirlwinds had flown into the ground. P/O Kitchener was fortunate that he was flying down a valley to the right of the hill on which Smith and Vine crashed.

On the RAF accident record card, dated 27 February 1941, it states that both aircraft had still not been found. It was not until 9 March that the bodies and wreckage of the missing Whirlwinds P6975 (Smith) and P6978 (Vine) were discovered on Green Hill - well away from the Bovey Tracey area where the search would have been concentrated. After January's heavy snowfall began to thaw, a farmer on horseback checking his sheep discovered the grim remains.

The two pilots were buried side by side in Exeter Higher Cemetery, one on 13 March and the other the following day.

The remains of the wreckage would have been recovered by 67 MU using horse pulled sledges to get it to a track near Huntingdon Warren from where it would have been taken away by lorries.

It is interesting that Kitchener, who remember was flying on the right side of the section, recalled the red flash on his right before pulling up. Did this mean that the two other Whirlwinds had cut across him in the murk and could have nearly collided with him?

Trouble seemed to happen to Whirlwinds in pairs. P/O J. H. Hoskins died on 9 October 1941 returning from flight formation practice when his 263 Squadron Whirlwind collided with another near Bath and two weeks later S/Ldr Johnny Sample DFC, CO of 137 Squadron, died when he baled out too low after his Whirlwind collided with another near Bath.

Whirlwind pilots (left to right) P/O Donald Vine, F/Lt Wynford Smith, unknown (anon)

DATE:	21 MARCH 1941
LOCATION/AREA:	HAMEL DOWN
AIRCRAFT TYPE:	H.P HAMPDEN MKI
SERIAL NO:	X3054
SQD/UNIT:	49 SQD / CODE EA / 5 GROUP
BASE:	SCAMPTON
TIME OF CRASH:	22.50HRS
CREW:	P/O THE HON ROBERT WILSON SGT RICHARD ELLIS SGT CHARLES LYON SGT RONALD BRAMES
PURPOSE OF FLIGHT:	LAYING MINES OFF LORIENT
CAUSE OF CRASH:	RADIO U/S AND BAD WEATHER

NOTES: The crew had problems with the radio during the return flight and were not able to fix their position. In bad weather, they were too low over high ground and crashed into the hillside. The pilot, P/O Wilson, was the only survivor, but he died of his injuries the next day.

His mother had a memorial stone placed at the crash site with the crew's initials on and many years later the Torbay Aircrew Association had a plaque fixed to the other side of the stone.

The inner harbour at Lorient today

HAMEL DOWN HAMPDEN

The crash site of Handley Page Hampden X3054 on Hamel Down, near Widecombe-in-the-Moor, is the best known of all the crash sites on Dartmoor because it is easy to find, being close to a road at Natsworthy Gate, and because of the large memorial stone placed there.

I have three small pieces from this crash, including a buckle from an oxygen mask worn by one of the crew. There is nothing to be found now and few would know that a 49 Squadron bomber crashed there on the night of Friday 21 March 1941 but for the memorial.

It was erected at the request of Lady Marjorie Wilson, whose 25 year-old son, P/O the Hon Robert David Wilson, died from his injuries the day after the crash. The other crew members, Sgt Richard Leonard Ashburton Ellis, 23, the co-pilot acting as navigator; Sgt Charles John Lyon, 23, the wireless operator and Sgt Ronald Brames, 22, the rear gunner, were killed in the crash. Sgt Ellis was on his first operation with the squadron.

The stone, with a cross, the RAF Squadron number and the initials of the crew carved on it, was placed roughly on the spot where the cockpit came to rest after the bomber broke up and caught fire. The pilot was pulled from the cockpit barely alive by local people, but he died the next day in hospital, after being operated on, without regaining consciousness.

The Hampden comes to grief (Author's interpretation)

The crew's initials on the granite memorial at the crash site and the plaque (opposite) on the other side

This explains the discrepancy on the back of the memorial where the now defunct Torbay and District Aircrew Association arranged in 1991 for a plaque to be fixed dedicated not only to the "selfless courage" of the Hampden crew but also that of their fellow airmen who perished on the moor during the war years. The plaque gives the date of 22 March, which was when P/O Wilson died, while the stone carving says 21.3.41, which was the correct day of the crash.

P/O Wilson was the son of Charles H. W. Wilson CB, DSO, 2nd Baron Nunburnholme, of the city of Kingston-upon-Hull. P/O Wilson and his South African born navigator, Sgt Ellis, are buried side by side at Exeter Higher Cemetery.

Sgt Lyon was buried in Prescott Cemetery, Lancashire, and Sgt Brames in Eltham (St John the Baptist) churchyard in London.

Sgt Lyon was always known as Ben by his 49 Squadron colleagues after the American Ben Lyon who featured in the popular BBC radio show called *Hi, Gang!*

Hampden X3054 was the only one of six aircraft from RAF Scampton in Lincolnshire not to return from the mine-laying mission off Lorient, southern Brittany, home to a major U-boat base. The crew had problems with their radio on the return flight and are believed to have come down through thick cloud to try to pinpoint their position, not realising they were over high ground.

Being so close to a road, all the wreckage was removed - not buried on site – much of it by a local girl driving a tractor.

In his splendid book "Uncle Tom Cobley and All: The Book of Widecombe-in-the-Moor", author Stephen Woods has this from Dorothy Baty (nee Miners): "A plane crashed on Hameldown and I had to go up with the tractor and tow a lot of the wreckage back. It was a bit of a trek as I had to miss all the big rocks on the way. I must have been 18 or 19 at the time."

ON 22ND MARCH 1941
A ROYAL AIR FORCE BOMBER
49 SQDN SCAMPTON
CRASHED RETURNING FROM
OPERATIONS OVER FRANCE
THE 4 CREW WERE LOST

THIS MEMORIAL BEARS
THEIR INITIALS AND SQUADRON
NUMBER - COMMEMORATING
THEIR SELFLESS COURAGE
AND THAT OF FELLOW AIRMEN
WHO PERISHED ON DARTMOOR
1939 - 1945
THEIR SACRIFICE HELPED US
TO MAINTAIN FREEDOM.

THE AIRCREW ASSOCIATION 1991.

DATE:	4 APRIL 1941
LOCATION/AREA:	HANGINGSTONE HILL
AIRCRAFT TYPE:	H.P HAMPDEN
SERIAL NO:	AD748
SQD/UNIT:	83 SQD / CODE OL / 5 GROUP
BASE:	SCAMPTON
TIME OF CRASH:	02.00HRS
CREW:	F/LT REG THOMPSON P/O LESLIE EVANS SGT ALAN MURRAY SGT LESLIE EDEN
PURPOSE OF FLIGHT:	LAYING MINES
CAUSE OF CRASH:	BAD WEATHER

NOTES:

On their return from France, the crew flew into fog. The pilot decided to land at St Eval in Cornwall but overflew and was probably making for Exeter when the Hampden hit the high ground. All the crew were killed.

Hangingstone Hill where the Hampden came down

A PROMISE KEPT

Just as he had promised, Leslie Evans was present when his wife Phyllis gave birth to their first child. Phyllis said she saw him – she did not know at the time that he had died the day before on Dartmoor.

P/O Evans was the navigator of Hampden AD748 OL-M which crashed near the top of Hangingstone Hill (1,948ft) at 02.00hrs on 4 April 1941 while returning from a minelaying mission off La Rochelle, France.

The cause of the crash has never been determined for certain, but the accident card suggests that the plotting charts used by navigators at that time gave the height of hills and mountains in metres rather than feet and this could have led the crew to believe they were well above the high ground. The bomber struck the hill around the 590m contour line shown on the current OS map.

Those killed along with P/O Evans were the pilot, F/Lt Reginald Thompson; the wireless operator, Sgt Alan Murray, and the air gunner, Sgt Leslie Eden.

The 83 Squadron Hampden took off from RAF Scampton, Lincolnshire, at 18.45hrs on 3 April 1941 as part of a force of six Hampdens to drop mines in the shipping channels off La

Promise kept – P/O Leslie Evans
(David Keast)

Rochelle. The RAF's codename for these operations was Gardening. The areas to be mined were given further codenames: Cinnamon was La Rochelle.

Two other Hampden squadrons of five aircraft each, 49 also from Scampton, and 144 from Hemswell (Lincs), were tasked with Gardening operations off Brest and La Pallice from where U-boats and Italian submarines operated. Brest also sheltered the German pocket battleships Scharnhorst and Gneisenau and the cruiser Prinz Eugen at this time.

Laying mines was a complex operation as well as a dangerous one, but F/Lt Thompson carried it out successfully and turned for home.

For the Hampden crews the most difficult part of their mission was still to come as a band of low cloud had settled over much of southern England and diversion to another airfield became necessary.

A few hours before, the Cornish airfield of St Eval had been visited by German fighter bombers who had dropped eight bombs before going on to attack nearby RNAS St Merryn. There were no fatalities but there had been some damage although not to the runways.

A Handley Page Hampden - you can see why it was known as the Flying Panhandle

It turned out to be quite a night for St Eval as at least three of the Hampden pilots had selected the airfield for their diversionary landing. First in was Hampden AD783, of 144 Squadron, whose hydraulics failed as a result of which the bomber overshot the runway and crashed in a field close by.

Grave of Sgt Alan Murray at Exeter Higher Cemetery

At 01.45hrs, came P4403 from 49 Squadron, piloted by Sgt Ball, who overshot on landing and hit a hedge. Both crews escaped injury.

Hampden AD748 had been fixed over the Lizard and F/Lt Thompson must have thought he was near the airfield when he began his descent through the murk and ploughed into Hangingstone Hill.

At 02.10hrs, it was realised the Hampden had crashed somewhere and at first light, a Lysander from Harrowbeer took off to try to find the missing bomber without success. It was two days later that a farmer checking on his sheep found the bodies and wreckage.

P/O Evans, the navigator, had been an

engineer before the war and in February 1940 he married his wife Phyllis and she was expecting their first child at the time of the crash.

He had promised his wife that whatever else happened, he would be present at the birth and when she gave birth to son Richard at a nursing home near Lincoln Cathedral, she had a vision of her husband, not knowing he was already dead.

P/O Evans had been with 83 Squadron for a month. He is buried at Scampton village St John the Baptist churchyard.

Sgt Eden is buried at Camberwell New Cemetery, Southwark, and Sgt Murray at Exeter Higher Cemetery.

The pilot, F/Lt Thompson, who came from Boars Hill in Oxfordshire, is buried at St Leonard's churchyard in Sunningwell. Within six months of his death, his father died of a broken heart.

The French port of Brest, 1941. The Scharnhorst *and* Gneisenau *berthed (upper left). The submarine pens (top middle and beneath cloud). On a clear day they looked an easy target.*

DATE:	20 APRIL 1941
LOCATION/AREA:	FOLLY GATE, NEAR OKEHAMPTON
AIRCRAFT TYPE:	H.P HARROW
SERIAL NO:	K7015
SQD/UNIT:	271 SQD / CODE BJ / 5 GROUP
BASE:	DONCASTER
TIME OF CRASH:	18.00HRS APPROX
CREW:	F/SGT M.E.PRICE P/O EDWARD PROCYK AC2 KENNETH MOORE AC1 KENNETH BEEVERS AC KENNETH ROBBINS
PURPOSE OF FLIGHT:	DELIVERING PARTS
CAUSE OF CRASH:	PORT ENGINE CAUGHT FIRE, BURNING THROUGH FLYING CONTROLS

NOTES:

Local policemen rescued F/Sgt Price, the pilot, but the other crew members were all killed.

The site is now buried under a silage clamp.

At 30, Polish P/O Edward Procyk was the oldest member of the crew (Polish Institute and Sikorski Museum)

The grave of P/O Edward Procyk at Exeter Cemetery

K7015 – ONE OF A HUNDRED

Two local policemen saved the life of the only survivor of a crash which killed four other crew members of a transport aircraft. But why the rescued pilot had not put the stricken K7015 Harrow down on the grass airfield at Folly Gate, Devon, remains a mystery.

The Handley Page Harrow was a large twin engine monoplane built from a metal frame covered with fabric. At 82ft long and a wing span of 88ft, with fixed undercarriage, it was an ugly and ungainly aircraft.

With a top speed of 200mph and cruising speed of 163mph, the Harrow was too slow for a bomber so it was used mainly as a transport aircraft and to train bomber crews. The first flight of a Harrow was made on 10 October 1936 and it is easy to understand why only 100 were built – 39 Mk I and the rest Mk II. The Harrow of this story was 62nd off the assembly line.

Pc Arthur Lemon, pictured outside a sandbagged Okehampton Police Station, helped rescue the pilot (Simon Dell Collection)

Allotted to 115 Squadron on 17 November 1937, K7015 stayed with them until 23 May 1939 when she was flown to RAF Warmwell in Dorset, which was home to 24 Maintenance Unit. Here she stayed until 14 October 1940 when 271 Squadron at Doncaster took delivery. This same day, K7015 was involved in an accident, but was repaired on site. Not a good omen for what was to follow.

On 20 April 1941, F/Sgt M. E. Price and his crew flew to St Eval in Cornwall to deliver spare aircraft parts. In the right-hand second pilot's seat sat P/O Edward Procyk, who had trained as an observer before the war and then retrained to become a pilot. This was his first flight with 271 Squadron and, at 30 years of age, he was the oldest member of the crew.

The rest of the crew all had Kenneth as their Christian name. There was AC1 Robbins from Manchester, AC2 Moore from Slough, who was the wireless operator, and AC1 Beevers from Harrogate.

The return flight to their base at Colerne in Wiltshire should have taken them about an hour, but as they flew over the edge of Dartmoor, the port Bristol Pegasus engine caught fire. The flames then spread to the fabric covered wing.

It seems odd that F/Sgt Price did not attempt to land at Folly Gate for as he flew over the airfield, the control cables burnt through, the aircraft flipped over onto its back and dived into a nearby wood. All the crew were killed apart from the injured pilot who was thrown out by the impact and then dragged away from the flames by local police constables Arthur Lemon and Trevor Moss, who saw the crash.

A large crowd soon gathered and when the land owner Mr Stanbury returned from evening chapel he was shocked to see a burning aircraft and lots of people on his land.

P/O Procyk and AC2 Moore are buried at Exeter Higher Cemetery while the other crew members were buried in their home towns.

Many years ago, with the permission of the land owner, I visited the site, which was covered with a silage clamp. However, by the edge of the wood, four small pieces of the Harrow were recovered, two of which bore Handley Page stamps

The crash site of the Harrow is now beneath a silage clamp.

Fire in the port engine brings disaster (Author's interpretation)

Pieces from the ill-fated Harrow

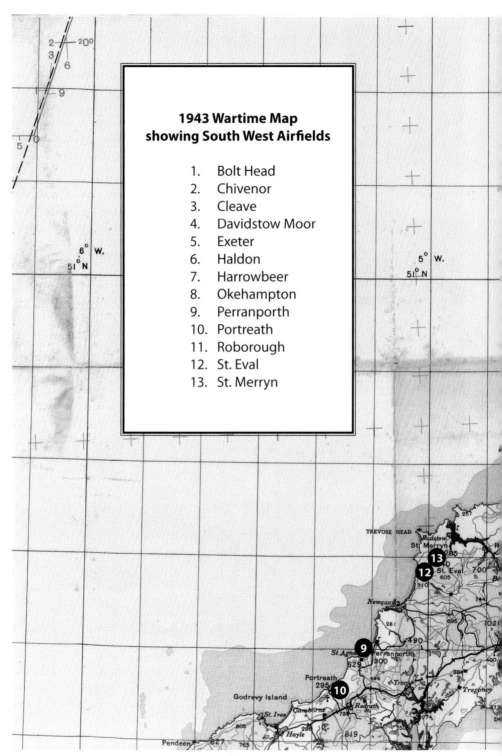

**1943 Wartime Map
showing South West Airfields**

1. Bolt Head
2. Chivenor
3. Cleave
4. Davidstow Moor
5. Exeter
6. Haldon
7. Harrowbeer
8. Okehampton
9. Perranporth
10. Portreath
11. Roborough
12. St. Eval
13. St. Merryn

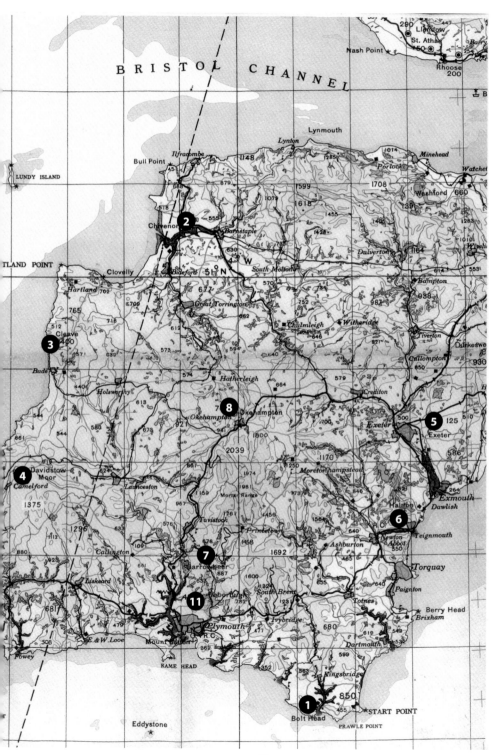

DATE:	19 MAY 1941
LOCATION/AREA:	BURRATOR
AIRCRAFT TYPE:	JUNKERS JU88 A.5
SERIAL NO:	5213 / 7T + AH
SQD/UNIT:	1/KUF 606
BASE:	LANNION, FRANCE
TIME OF CRASH:	02.36HRS
CREW:	Uffz PAUL NOWACKI Oberlt zur See GUNTHER HITSCHFELD Uffz JOACHIM KASTEN Uffz HANS KNOR
PURPOSE OF FLIGHT:	ATTACK ON SHIPPING IN IRISH SEA
CAUSE OF CRASH:	HIT LEATHER TOR

NOTES:

1/KUF 606, using Ju88s for the first time on operation, had a disastrous night and this was one of their aircraft that failed to return. After hitting near the top of Leather Tor, the Ju88 crashed near the road by Burrator Reservoir. All the crew were killed.

The Walther flare pistol found on top of Leather Tor. The cartridge shown for comparison is from another crash site in Devon. This was a standard piece of equipment on German bombers. It was made of steel, whereas fighter flare pistols were made of lightweight alloy.

BURRATOR JU88

The mysterious crash of a German raider on Dartmoor in 1941 provided the RAF with valuable information about a new armament.

The four-man crew of the Ju88, from 1/KUF 606, a German Coastal Command squadron, were all killed in the early hours of 19 May when their aircraft crashed and exploded near Burrator Reservoir while returning from an attack on shipping in the Irish Sea.

It proved a disastrous night for the squadron, which was using Ju88s on operations for the first time. As well as the Burrator aircraft, the Germans lost Hptm Wolf Beitzke and his crew when shot down by AA fire over Falmouth harbour; Lt Werner Neudeck died when he crashed 6km west of Thury Harcourt, Calvados, one crew member was fatally injured, one badly injured and one lightly injured; Oblt Helmut Eiermann and another member of his crew were killed and two injured when he crashed at their Lannion base in northern Brittany and Oblt Peter Schnoor belly-landed back at Lannion with 25 per cent damage.

The pilot of the Dartmoor Ju88 was Uffz Paul Nowaki. With him were Oblt zur See Günther Hitschfeld, Uffz Joachim Kasten and Uffz Hans Knör. At 02.36hrs on the morning of 19 May, their aircraft hit Leather Tor. The lower gondola was torn off, along with both airscrews. The aircraft became a glider for quarter of

RAF experts examine the burnt out wreck of the Ju88 (via Peter Foote)

The Home Guard stands guard over the Ju88 wreck to prevent looting. Sheeps Tor is in the background (via Peter Foote)

a mile until it crashed through stone walls, coming to rest 50 yards from the narrow road beside the reservoir where it exploded and burnt out leaving just the tailplane.

Police from Tavistock put a guard on the aircraft until RAF investigators arrived next day to remove the bodies and check over the wreckage. They discovered that the German aircraft had been fitted with an anti-shipping 20mm nose cannon – the first found on any Ju88.

They also found a single .303 strike in the tailplane. This could have come from a ship's machine gun as no British night fighter reported any contact with Ju88s over Devon for this night.

The Burrator Ju88, work number 5213, had been built by the Allgemeine Transport Works, Leipzig, in February 1941. The aircraft was painted green/grey splinter on the upper surfaces with pale blue lower surfaces. On the fuselage, the code letters/numbers 7T AH were painted black with the A outlined in white.

Formed in Norway, 1/KUF 606 technically operated under the Kriegsmarine (German War Navy). One of the dead from this Ju88 was an Oblt zur See, which was the equivalent of a sub lieutenant in our Royal Navy.

Some years ago, a man walking near Leather Tor found the badly rusted flare pistol from the Ju88 among the rocks. It was passed to me for my collection and is now on display, with a few other pieces from the crash, at the RAF Memorial Museum, Davidstow Moor, Cornwall.

Ju88 in flight (Deutsches Bundesarchiv)

DATE:	9 JUNE 1941
LOCATION/AREA:	ROBOROUGH AIRFIELD
AIRCRAFT TYPE:	PERCIVAL PROCTOR
SERIAL NO:	P6256
SQD/UNIT:	16 SQD / CODE EG
BASE:	WESTONZOYLAND
TIME OF CRASH:	17.30HRS
CREW:	W/CDR RICHARD C. HANCOCK PLUS GROUND CREW PASSENGER
PURPOSE OF FLIGHT:	UNKNOWN
CAUSE OF CRASH:	UNKNOWN

NOTES:

W/Cdr Hancock was taking off from Roborough when, for some reason, the Proctor crashed and caught fire. The ground crew passenger escaped with minor burns, but the pilot suffered multiple injuries and died in the Royal Naval Hospital at Plymouth at 13.30hrs the following day. He was 39 and is buried at Lustleigh.

A Percival Proctor (RAF Museum)

W/Cdr Richard Hancock (courtesy of Lustleigh Community Archive and the Gould Family)

DATE:	7 AUGUST 1941
LOCATION/AREA:	ASHBURTON
AIRCRAFT TYPE:	HAWKER HURRICANE IIA
SERIAL NO:	Z2677
SQD/UNIT:	316 (POLISH) SQD / CODE SZ, 10 GROUP
BASE:	PEMBURY, SOUTH WALES
TIME OF CRASH:	11.40HRS
CREW:	P/O FRANCISZEK KOZLOWSKI
PURPOSE OF FLIGHT:	PATROL
CAUSE OF CRASH:	LOST AILERON CONTROL

*Franciszek Kozlowski
as Sergeant*

NOTES: After losing aileron control, the elevators continued to function so P/O Kozlowski climbed his Hurricane to 8,000ft. The aircraft rolled over and spiralled slowly down and the pilot baled out.

The court of inquiry said he should have switched the engine off to prevent a fire. At the time of the accident, he had logged 500 flying hours, 230 on Hurricanes.

P/O Kozlowski had flown with the Polish Air Force before fleeing to France and then Britain. He flew in the Battle of Britain with 501 Sqd and was shot down on 18 August 1940 by Luftwaffe ace Oblt Gerhard Schopel. He baled out with a bullet wound in a leg. He later flew with 308 Sqd before moving to 316 Sqd.

This 25 year-old Polish hero, who was awarded the Polish Pilot Medal four times and the War Cross, was shot down and killed in Spitfire EN171 on 13 March 1943 while escorting American B17s. He is buried at Hautot-sur-Mer, Dieppe.

Many years later, the Merlin engine of P/O Kozlowski's Spitfire was recovered and put on display.

A Hawker Hurricane

DATE:	21 AUGUST 1941
LOCATION /AREA:	NEAR TAVISTOCK
AIRCRAFT TYPE:	WESTLAND LYSANDER MKI
SERIAL NO:	V9551
SQUAD/UNIT:	16 SQD/CODE KJ / 36 WING SOUTHERN COMMAND
BASE:	ROBOROUGH
TIME OF CRASH:	UNKNOWN
CREW:	P/O L.B. WILTON
PURPOSE OF FLIGHT:	NOT KNOWN
CAUSE OF CRASH:	ENGINE FAILURE

NOTES:

The aircraft report is of such poor quality that it is only possible to make out these few details and that the pilot baled out safely.

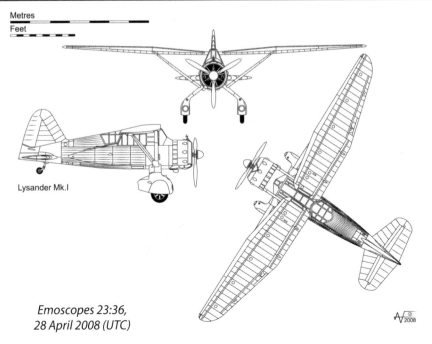

Metres

Feet

Lysander Mk.I

Emoscopes 23:36,
28 April 2008 (UTC)

Members of 16 Squadron pictured in 1940 in front of a Westland Lysander

DATE:	5 SEPTEMBER 1941
LOCATION/AREA:	HORRABRIDGE
AIRCRAFT TYPE:	VICKERS WELLINGTON MKIC
SERIAL NO:	W5684
SQD/UNIT:	115 SQD / CODE KO-G / 3 GROUP
BASE:	MARHAM, NORFOLK
TIME OF CRASH:	EARLY HOURS
CREW:	P/O SCHOLES SGT NEWARK SGT MORTON SGT KINSEY SGT BATTY SGT HAYNES
PURPOSE OF FLIGHT:	OPERATION TO BREST
CAUSE OF CRASH:	BAD WEATHER

NOTES: The Wellington took off at 20.03hrs the evening before to bomb Brest, but ran into bad weather on the return flight and the crew all baled out safely in the vicinity of Horrabridge.

The pilot, P/O John Scholes, was a Canadian serving in the RAF. He was promoted to Flight Lieutenant on 10 May 1943. He died on 28 December 1943, aged 32, in a flying accident and is buried at Bath. Sgt Morton was killed on 19 July 1944 when his Lancaster was shot down over Belgium. Sgt Batty and Sgt Haynes were crew members of a 115 Squadron Wellington shot down over Stuttgart on 7 May 1942. All the crew baled out, but insecure parachute webbing caused the deaths of Sgt Batty and the pilot, 23 year-old F/Lt John Sword, DFC AFC. Sgt Haynes was made a prisoner of war.

Men of 115 Squadron at Marham, Norfolk

DATE:	27 SEPTEMBER 1941
LOCATION/AREA:	HAMEL DOWN
AIRCRAFT TYPE:	BRISTOL BEAUFIGHTER MKIIF
SERIAL NO:	R2442
SQD/UNIT:	307 (POLISH) SQD / CODE EW/10 GROUP
BASE:	EXETER
TIME OF CRASH:	DAYTIME
CREW:	P/O W. GAYZLER P/O W. PFLEGER
PURPOSE OF FLIGHT:	DUMMY AIR TO GROUND ATTACKS
CAUSE OF CRASH:	LOW CLOUD

NOTES: This aircraft had twin Merlin engines and was used as a night fighter. It flew into the side of high ground at 1,400ft while descending through low cloud. P/O Witold Gayzler, who was the pilot, and his observer, P/O Wlodzimierz Pfleger, were both killed and are buried at Exeter Higher Cemetery.

P/O Witold Gayzler (back row, far left) and P/O Wlodzimierz Pfleger (far right) defended Exeter

This Polish squadron had moved to Exeter in April 1941 for the day and night defence of the town. Today, the Polish national flag is flown on Exeter Guildhall on 15 November each year as a tribute to 307 Squadron.

During the clear-up operation of the wreck, the salvage team are said to have rolled one of the Beaufighter's wheels down the hillside to collect on the way down. But they could not find it. Over the years I have looked for it without success. If you find it, I hope you will donate it to our museum at Davidstow Moor.

A MkIIF Bristol Beaufighter like the one which crashed at Hamel Down

DATE:	29 NOVEMBER 1941
LOCATION/AREA:	CRAMBER TOR
AIRCRAFT TYPE:	SUPERMARINE SPITFIRE MKVB
SERIAL NO:	W3968
SQD/UNIT:	317 (POLISH) SQD / CODE JH
BASE:	EXETER
TIME OF CRASH:	AFTER 10.35HRS
CREW:	P/O KAROL WOJCIK
PURPOSE OF FLIGHT:	SCRAMBLE
CAUSE OF CRASH:	DENSE CLOUD, RADIO U/S

NOTES:

Yellow section of three Spitfires was scrambled at 10.35hrs to intercept an enemy aircraft off Plymouth. P/O Wojcik failed to return after losing radio contact with the other two aircraft that returned to base. Six aircraft were sent to look for him without success.

The wreckage and body of the 24 year-old pilot were found the next day near Cramber Tor, north of Crazy Well Pool.

He was the first member of his squadron to be killed in action.

P/O Karol Wojcik, the first of his squadron to be killed (via Wilhelm Ratuszynski)

DATE:	18 DECEMBER 1941
LOCATION/AREA:	HARROWBEER AIRFIELD
AIRCRAFT TYPE:	SUPERMARINE SPITFIRE MK VB
SERIAL NO:	AD428
SQD/UNIT:	302 SQD (POLISH)
BASE:	HARROWBEER
TIME OF CRASH:	UNKNOWN
CREW:	S/LDR JULIAN KOWALSKI
PURPOSE OF FLIGHT:	PATROL
CAUSE OF CRASH:	SWUNG ON TAKE OFF

NOTES:

S/Ldr Julian Kowalski's Spitfire swung during take off and struck Spitfire AD555 killing Sgt Aleksander Przesmycki, a mechanic, who was attending to the parked Spitfire's magneto.

S/Ldr Kowalski was unhurt. Both aircraft were repaired.

The 302 Squadron's CO had been taking off for Operation Veracity I. He was to be part of the escort for bombers attempting to cripple the German warships Gneisenau and Scharnhorst in Brest Harbour.

He had a glittering career in the RAF and after demobilisation in 1947 settled in Ipswich where he died in December 1986.

S/Ldr Julian Kowalski
(Polish Institute and Sikorski Museum)

DATE:	27 DECEMBER 1941
LOCATION/AREA:	BUCKFASTLEIGH
AIRCRAFT TYPE:	VICKERS WELLINGTON MKIC
SERIAL NO:	Z8971
SQD/UNIT:	75 SQD / CODE AA
BASE:	FELTWELL, NORFOLK
TIME OF CRASH:	20.00HRS
CREW:	SGT MACHIN SGT THOMPSON SGT BUCKBY SGT BOLSHAW SGT CLEMENTS SGT BOURNE
PURPOSE OF FLIGHT:	BOMBING BREST U-BOAT PENS
CAUSE OF CRASH:	ENGINE FAILURE & BAD WEATHER

NOTES: The Wellington had taken off at 16.26hrs to bomb the U-boat pens at Brest. The port engine failed at 19.39hrs during the return flight when the aircraft made landfall at Dawlish. Exeter airfield was lit, but for some reason the aircraft ended up over Dartmoor.

The crew baled out at 2,000ft and most came down around Buckfastleigh. The rear gunner, Sgt Bourne, ended up in hospital at Newton Abbot.

A 75 (NZ) Squadron Wellington at Feltwell

BALE OUT!

A sergeant pilot had already cheated death once. Four months later he was put to the test again when his battle-damaged bomber lumbered through a cloudy night sky over Dartmoor.

Two days after Christmas in 1941, 12 Vickers Wellington IC long range medium bombers of 75 Squadron took off at 16.26hrs from their Norfolk base at Feltwell to attack targets at Brest and Dusseldorf. Among the four aircraft tasked with the French part of the mission was Z8971, skippered by a young sergeant called Harry Machin.

He had been the second pilot to P/O Alf Raphael during raids on Cologne, Dunkirk, Ostend docks, Frankfurt, Brest and Hamburg, but a botched attempt to bomb Berlin almost proved his last mission.

On 20 September 1941, P/O Raphael in Wellington T2085 had taken off with 73 other aircraft to bomb Berlin and Ostend, but soon after take-off the raid was cancelled because of worsening weather. However, not all aircraft received the recall and continued to the target.

Twelve Wellingtons were either abandoned by their crews in the thick fog or crash landed. P/O Raphael's aircraft, with Sgt Machin aboard, landed heavily in a field at Horning, nine miles from Norwich, and observer Robert Craig was seriously injured. He died in hospital the next day.

So Sgt Machin had one narrow escape and now he had his own crew to lead for this Saturday night raid on the Brest U-boat pens. The second pilot was Sgt Thompson, the navigator Sgt W. E. Buckley, the radio operator Sgt Bolshaw and the two gunners were Sgt Clements and Sgt Bourne.

There was heavy flak as usual over Brest, but Sgt Machin released his bomb load before heading for home. At 19.39hrs the port engine failed and the pilot knew he would never reach Norfolk so Sgt Bolshaw put out a call for help.

RAF Exeter answered, but told them the weather over Devon was poor with cloud from ground to 8,000ft. However, they would light the airfield when Z8971 made landfall in the hope that it would help Sgt Machin make a safe landing.

At 19.54hrs, the Wellington reached the coast at Dawlish, but the crew were unable to spot the Exeter runway lights and Sgt Machin decided to give the bale out order. While he kept the Wellington steady, the crew jumped from 2,000ft and then Sgt Machin baled out too.

He came down at Staverton, near Totnes, and telephoned Exeter at 20.45hrs to tell them what had happened and that he was about to search for his crew.

By 21.15hrs, 3 Group reported that all the crew were safe. One of them turned up at a hotel at Buckfastleigh slightly injured and it was later reported that the rear gunner, Sgt Bourne, was in hospital at Newton Abbot.

The next day, RAF Feltwell asked RAF Exeter to pick up four members of the crew from Buckfastleigh and take them back to Exeter as the station commander would be flying down in the afternoon to pick them up. This was the crew's final operation with the squadron.

As for the abandoned Wellington, it came down on Dartmoor, but I have never found where.

U-Boat pens at Brest, France

(Jiří Rajlich)

U-Boats berthed in pens awaiting action

(Jiří Rajlich)

*The words 'valley fog' were underlined - see **Hamel Down Carpetbagger** story on page 131. Typical conditions on Dartmoor which caused many problems for pilots.*

DATE:	7 JANUARY 1942
LOCATION/AREA:	HOLNE
AIRCRAFT TYPE:	MESSERSCHMITT ME-109-E7
SERIAL NO:	W/N 4970
SQD/UNIT:	1 (F) 123 RECONNAISSANCE UNIT
BASE:	MAUPERTUS, FRANCE
TIME OF CRASH:	10.50HRS
CREW:	UFFZ KURT THUNE
PURPOSE OF FLIGHT:	PHOTO RECCE
CAUSE OF CRASH:	ENGINE FAILURE

NOTES: This was the last Me-109 to crash on mainland Britain. Unteroffizier Thune had to bale out from 6,000ft when his engine cut out during a photo reconnaissance mission over Plymouth, Devonport and Exeter. He landed about a mile and a half away from his crashed aircraft and was quickly captured.

The crash site at Lakemoor Wood

THE LUCKY ONE

The last Me-109 to crash on mainland Britain saw an unwelcome guest drop in on the Dartmoor village of Holne, but it was as a welcome guest that Kurt Thune dropped in 50 years later.

German reconnaissance pilot Unteroffizier Thune had to bale out of his stricken aircraft from 6,000ft when his photographic mission along the Devon coast went badly wrong. He landed safely near the village of Holne and was promptly taken prisoner by some of the locals while his Messerschmitt plummeted into the edge of a nearby wood.

Air intelligence officials soon converged on the crash site to recover the aircraft's camera equipment and film in a bid to discover just what Unteroffizier Thune, of the 1 Staffel-Fernaufklaerungsgruppe 123, had been up to.

Unteroffizier Kurt Thune prisoner of war

On Wednesday 7 January 1942, Thune had taken off in Me-109E-7 from Maupertus with another aircraft on a similar mission and set course for the Devon coast. At some stage the other 109 pilot left to carry out his part of the mission. Thune reached Plymouth and photographed Devonport Dockyard and the city. He then flew on towards Exeter to photograph the town, but the boost pressure dropped and the engine stalled. Twice Thune managed to restart the engine but it cut out a third time, and then with oil fumes entering the cockpit, the 22 year-old pilot decided he had to bale out.

He landed and was arrested by Rodney Bickle and one of the local Home Guard members, Jim Axford, and put in a pick-up truck belonging to Lew Perkins, who had to stop work on a wall he was building to drive them to Ashburton Police Station. Lew had a moan later that he was not compensated for the precious fuel he had used.

So the young, blond German disappeared from Holne, but he was not forgotten

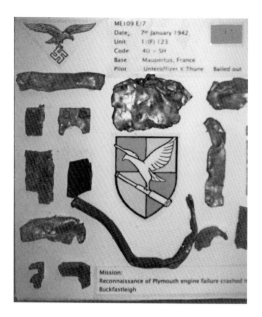

ME109 E/7
Date, 7th January 1942
Unit 1/(F) 123
Code 4U + SH
Base Maupertus, France
Pilot Unteroffizier K Thune   Bailed out

Mission:
Reconnaissance of Plymouth engine failure crashed
Buckfastleigh

A few parts from the crash site

by the locals and after the war many wrote to him at his home at Stassfurt in East Germany. However, it was not until after the fall of the Berlin Wall that Kurt Thune was able to reply.

Retired Royal Navy officer and local historian Hubert Fox was then instrumental in organising a reunion which brought Kurt back to the village in 1992, 50 years after his parachute drop. Kurt was accompanied by his wife, Edith. The reunion was held at Langaford in Holne, where Lew Perkins had been building the wall when he was asked to drive the German prisoner to Ashburton. By then it was the home of Mr Fox.

During his visit, Kurt had tea with Elsie Kennard, the widow of the late Jim Axford, at her home at Buckfastleigh, and the former pilot was able to solve a mystery which had puzzled Mrs Kennard for half a century. She had been told about pieces of paper which he had thrown out of the back of the van as he was driven away. What were they? Kurt told her through his translator that it was his pilot's licence, documents and flight plan. Why he was not searched at the time of his arrest or why his escort did not stop to pick up the papers is unclear. The pilot would also have been carrying his personal Luger pistol and would have had a flare gun strapped to his right leg for firing the signal of the day on being challenged when preparing to land. Kurt had surrendered a knife and the flare pistol when arrested, but his possession of a prized Luger is not mentioned anywhere so perhaps Kurt threw it away and it is lying around somewhere.

Kurt told the guests at his reunion, which was reported on by the Western Morning News, that he was treated well by his captors.

He said: "The police gave me a cup of tea and I handed around my cigarettes to them. It was so confusing and exciting."

He was kept several hours in the police station at Ashburton before being moved to Cambridgeshire. He later spent four years as a prisoner of war in Canada.

After jettisoning his cockpit canopy, Uffz Kurt Thune
is about to bale out (Author's interpretation)

His Me-109E crashed into the corner of a field on the edge of Lakemoor Wood. There is nothing to see there now, not even a hollow in the ground. A reconnaissance aircraft was a valuable find for the authorities and the wreckage was quickly salvaged. In the 70s and 80s, the site was investigated again by various groups, one with a mechanical digger, but little was found.

Kurt had already survived one crash four months before when his Me-109E crash landed and overturned on returning from another recce flight. When Kurt failed to return from his Devon mission, Uffz Rolf Grossberger replaced him, but on Friday 24 April 1942, he crashed into the sea off the Isle of Wight. His body was washed ashore five weeks later. Kurt Thune was the lucky one.

Kurt Thune back for tea
(Western Morning News)

DATE:	10 JANUARY 1942
LOCATION/AREA:	NUTLEY FARM, NORTH OF MOORSHOP
AIRCRAFT TYPE:	VICKERS WELLINGTON
SERIAL NO:	W5682
SQD/UNIT:	311 (CZECH) SQD / CODE KX-Y
BASE:	EAST WRETHAM, NORFOLK
TIME OF CRASH:	18.15HRS
CREW:	SGT JIRI FINA SGT KAREL MAZUREK F/O KAREL SLAMA SGT FRANTISEK RAJSKUP SGT FRANTISEK SIPULA SGT JOSEF SVOBODA
PURPOSE OF FLIGHT:	BOMBING BREST HARBOUR
CAUSE OF CRASH:	ENGINE FAILURE

NOTES:

Half way to the target, the port engine caught fire and the bombs were jettisoned. The bomber, with the flames extinguished, turned for home and after reaching the coast it came in for an emergency landing in a field, but hit trees and then a haystack before breaking in half. All the crew survived.

This squadron was formed as a heavy bomber squadron in July 1940 from Czech airmen who escaped to Britain.

311 Squadron Wellingtons in flight (Jiří Rajlich)

HAYSTACK WELLINGTON

The six man crew of a Wellington bomber survived a spectacular crash on Dartmoor, but within seven months four of them were dead and the two other crew members had each survived another brush with death.

Problems began for Sgt Jiri Fina and his 311 (Czech) Squadron crew during a Saturday night raid on the northern Finistere port of Brest. They had left their Norfolk base at East Wretham at 3.40hrs on 10 January 1942, but on their way to the target, and approximately halfway across the English Channel, Sgt Karel Mazurek, the second pilot, suddenly noticed that the left engine was misfiring. Gradually the Wellington began to lose altitude.

The captain, Sgt Fina, took over the controls, but still the Wellington lost height. When the aircraft was down to only 1,000m above sea level, Sgt Fina decided to jettison his bombload and abort the mission.

Almost as soon as he had turned back, the faulty engine caught fire and although the crew managed to extinguish the blaze with balls of white foam from the engine's fire extinguishing equipment, the captain told his crew to be ready for a possible landing in the sea.

Through brilliant airmanship, Sgt Fina managed to nurse the by now shaking Wellington back to England, making landfall west of Plymouth. However, as he was coming down to make an emergency landing in a field, the rear end of the fuselage struck a tree and then one of the wings caught on a large haystack.

71

*Pilot Sgt Jiri Fina
(Jiří Rajlich)*

The big bomber was spun 180 degrees and crashed heavily. The fuselage split in half and the rear end, with the gunner Sgt Frantisek Rajskup still in his turret, flew over the rest of the aircraft and landed some 20 metres ahead of it. Miraculously, he and the rest of the crew survived.

The only injury was to the navigator, F/O Karel Slama, who suffered two broken vertebrae. Sgt Rajskup had only light injuries, but Sgt Fina, Sgt Mazurek, Sgt Frantisek Sipula and Sgt Josef Svoboda were unhurt.

It was 06.15hrs and the Wellington had come down at Nutley Farm, north of Moorshop and 5k east of Tavistock. The fact that the aircraft did not catch fire, saved the lives of the crew – but their luck was not to last.

Sgt Svoboda was the first to be killed that same year. He was the wireless operator on Wellington Z1070 which went missing from an operation to attack the Renault factory at Boulogne-Billancourt on 1 March. The aircraft came down in the area of Creil and all six on board were killed.

Then on the night of 12 March, during a raid on Kiel, Wellington R1802 with Sgt Fina at the controls and Sgt Rajskup in the rear turret went missing over the North Sea. The aircraft sent an SOS at 20.53hrs and later a message saying it was going to ditch. Co-ordinates were given, but a Hampden searched the area for 3hrs 20min without finding any trace of the bomber or crew.

Sgt Sipula was the next to go. He was in Wellington DV665 on 18 August when it reported it was being attacked by enemy fighters. Nothing more was heard from the six man crew.

That left just Sgt Mazurek, the second pilot of the Dartmoor Wellington, and F/O Slama, who was the navigator that day.

*Second Pilot Sgt Karel Mazurek
receiving his DFM (Jiří Rajlich)*

F/O Slama was among the crew of S/Ldr Joseph Sejbl's Wellington HF921 which came under heavy attack from four Ju88s on 29 September, 20k south of Land's End, during an anti-submarine patrol. The nose gunner, Sgt Pavel Friedlander, was badly wounded and was unable to escape when the Wellington ditched in the sea.

The crew spent a night in the dinghy before being picked up the next day suffering from exposure and various injuries.

F/O Slama later underwent pilot and fighter pilot training and joined 313 Squadron. I believe he survived the war.

Sgt Josef Svoboda
Wireless Operator,
(Jiří Rajlich)

Sgt Mazurek, too, lived to see peace but not before another escape which earned him a DFM.

He was the captain of Wellington HD998 which was attacked by four Ju88s while on patrol on 11 September. Due to his skilful flying and aggressive shooting by the gunners – two of the enemy planes were damaged – Sgt Mazurek was able to escape into cloud cover.

Refuelling a 311 Squadron Wellington at East Wretham (Jiří Rajlich)

DATE:	27 JANUARY 1942
LOCATION/AREA:	PRINCETOWN
AIRCRAFT TYPE:	LOCKHEED HUDSON
SERIAL NO:	AM741
SQD/UNIT:	224 SQD / CODE QA
BASE:	ST EVAL
TIME OF CRASH:	11.09HRS
CREW:	S/LDR R.G LYNN SGT B.B WILLERTON F/SGT H C. LILEY SGT R.SCOTT SGT T.K. COOPER
PURPOSE OF FLIGHT:	ANTI SHIPPING OVER THE ENGLISH CHANNEL
CAUSE OF CRASH:	HIT BY ENEMY FIRE

NOTES: The Hudson was hit by return fire from a minesweeper and the starboard engine eventually seized. A Mayday was sent. All loose equipment was jettisoned and the pilot managed to get the aircraft up to 5,000ft and at 11.09hrs he reported they were over land and would bale out.

Loose equipment is thrown out of the Hudson to try to keep it in the air (Author's interpretation)

PRINCETOWN HUDSON

A Lockheed Hudson, which went looking for enemy shipping in the English Channel, ended up a wreck on the moor near Princetown.

Powered by two 1200hp Pratt and Whitney Wasp engines, the Hudson had an endurance time of six hours and 55 minutes and, with a range of 2,160 miles, it was ideally suited for a Coastal Command role.

Hudson AM741 had arrived at Liverpool Docks from America after being shipped from the Lockheed works, one of 350 of these aircraft delivered to the RAF by July 1941 through the lend-lease agreement negotiated by Roosevelt and Churchill.

The aircraft was taken on by 53 Squadron, based at St Eval, Cornwall, on 14 July 41 and remained with them until 19 December of that year when 224 Squadron, also based at the north Cornwall airfield, took her over. This squadron, originally based at Leuchars in Scotland, had been flying Hudsons since 1939 and were the first squadron to be equipped with the type. They had been flying patrols over the North Sea from day one of the Second World War.

On 27 January 1941, S/Ldr R.G. Lynn and his crew of Sgt B.B. Willerton, F/Sgt H.C. Liley, Sgt R. Scott and Sgt T.K. Cooper took off at 04.40hrs for an anti-shipping patrol over the English Channel. After passing over the Longships Lighthouse at 08.14hrs, they had seen only one local fishing vessel, so turned back on a reciprocal course.

At 09.00hrs, a message was received diverting the Hudson to Thorney Island and 40 minutes later, with visibility down to half a mile, the crew spotted three vessels. Then out of the murk an enemy minesweeper appeared and S/Ldr Lynn told the crew to make ready for the attack.

It was made from the port beam and at a height of 30ft. Four 250lb bombs were dropped, but no hits seen. The gunners on the minesweeper, however, caught their attacker with shells and bullets. Damage was caused to the rudder, a trimming wire had been cut, and the starboard engine began to leak oil. The Hudson had to break off the attack.

At 10.15hrs, the starboard engine seized and the crew had to begin the distress procedure. The wireless operator sent a message to base: "Flying at 4,000ft above cloud. Do you advise baling out over land?" Five minutes later a reply came back: "Can you make Thorney Island?"

At this time the starboard engine began to vibrate badly, threatening to take the mounting or wing with it. S/Ldr Lynn managed to get the Hudson to 5,000ft where the crew lightened the aircraft by jettisoning the unused bombs, loose equipment and surplus fuel.

At 10.30hrs, a message was sent to St Eval: "Baling out, nearest land." The reply came at 11.09hrs: "Over land, bale out."

At this point, S/Ldr Lynn ordered his crew to jump. He then switched off the port engine and baled out himself.

Hudson AM741 came down near Princetown and the crew landed safely nearby, although Sgt Cooper fractured a collar-bone and suffered cuts.

The remains of the Hudson were cleared away by 67 MU and nothing remains at the site today.

A German M-class minesweeper similar to the one which brought down the Princetown Hudson (Deutsches Bundesarchiv)

DATE:	7 FEBRUARY 1942
LOCATION/AREA:	CHUDLEIGH
AIRCRAFT TYPE:	WESTLAND LYSANDER MKIIIA
SERIAL NO:	V9292
SQD/UNIT:	16 SQD / CODE KJ/ 36 WING SOUTHERN COMMAND
BASE:	ROBOROUGH/ANDOVER
TIME OF CRASH:	14.00HRS
CREW:	P/O D.H. LEONARD
PURPOSE OF FLIGHT:	ARMY CO-OPERATION
CAUSE OF CRASH:	FUEL/BAD WEATHER

NOTES: Lost and very low on fuel, P/O Leonard attempted a forced landing, but the engine cut out and he crashed. He was unhurt but the Lysander was written off.

Westland Lysander

DATE:	15 MARCH 1942
LOCATION/AREA:	SHIPLEY TOR
AIRCRAFT TYPE:	SUPERMARINE SPITFIRE MKIV PRID
SERIAL NO:	BP890
SQD/UNIT:	1PRU / CODE LY
BASE:	BENSON, OXFORDSHIRE
TIME OF CRASH	DAYTIME
CREW:	P/O A.S.R.MACKENZIE (S.RHO)
PURPOSE OF FLIGHT:	FERRY FLIGHT TO MIDDLE EAST
CAUSE OF CRASH:	BAD WEATHER

NOTES:

P/O Angus Mackenzie, aged 27, from Southern Rhodesia, was on his way from Benson to St Eval in Cornwall where he was to refuel before flying to Gibraltar and then the Middle East. The aircraft struck Shipley Tor, near Shipley Bridge at 16.30hrs and the pilot was killed. He is buried in Exeter Higher Cemetery.

The headstone of P/O Mackenzie in Exeter

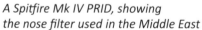

A Spitfire Mk IV PRID, showing the nose filter used in the Middle East

DATE:	8 MAY 1942
LOCATION/AREA:	MANATON
AIRCTRAFT TYPE:	SUPERMARINE SPITFIRE MK VB
SERIAL NO:	BL438
SQD/UNIT:	154 SQD/CODE HT
BASE:	FOWLMERE, EAST ANGLIA
TIME OF CRASH:	MORNING
CREW:	SGT JOHN OLIVER (RNZAF)
PURPOSE OF FLIGHT:	GUARDING ROYAL TRAIN
CAUSE OF CRASH:	UNKNOWN

NOTES:

King George VI and Queen Elizabeth were visiting Exeter
following heavy raids on the Devon capital and Sgt Oliver's
Spitfire was one of several guarding the Royal Train.
He was badly injured following a flying accident in the
Manaton area and the 27 year-old New Zealander died
later in Moretonhampstead military hospital. The cause
of the crash is unknown. The King and Queen had been to
Devonport the day before.

Looking towards Manaton Church from the
old miners' path

The headstone of Sgt John Oliver in Exeter

DATE:	24 MAY 1942
LOCATION/AREA:	STANDON HILL
AIRCRAFT TYPE:	AVRO LANCASTER MKI
SERIAL NO:	R5617
SQD/UNIT:	207 SQD / CODE EM / 5 GROUP
BASE:	BOTTESFORD, LINCS
TIME OF CRASH:	LATE EVENING
CREW:	SGT T.K. PAUL (RNZAF) SGT T. WHITEMAN SGT A.P. PATERSON SGT L. M .SMITH SGT R.L. MELLISH (RCAF) SGT C.A. PANKHURST
PURPOSE OF FLIGHT:	NIGHT CROSS-COUNTRY NAVIGATION EXERCISE
CAUSE OF CRASH:	BAD WEATHER

NOTES: During bad weather, the Lancaster crashed on Standon Hill, near Tavy Cleave. The pilot, Sgt Thomas Paul, and Sgt Thomas Whiteman were the only survivors. Sgt Paul was killed later in the war while flying a Wellington bomber with an OTU.

The Lancaster pancakes on to the hillside (Author's interpretation)

FIANCEE'S TRIBUTE TO DARTMOOR PILOT

A Lancaster crash on a Dartmoor hill in 1942 may have contributed to the death of the pilot and all but one of his crew during another training flight just over two years later.

That was the conclusion of an official inquiry into the loss of Wellington Z8793, which came down in a Buckinghamshire wood during a night bombing training exercise on Tuesday 4 January 1944.

The pilot of the aircraft was New Zealander W/O Thomas Paul, an instructor with No. 11 Operational Training Unit at RAF Westcott, Buckinghamshire.

New Zealander Sgt Thomas Paul, whose fiancée never forgot him

The crash of the Wellington into a wood on Farnham Common also claimed the lives of the second pilot, F/Sgt Arthur Coulter, 23; the navigator Sgt Ernest Clayton, 21; the wireless operator F/Sgt Jack O'Callaghan, 21, and one of the two air gunners, Sgt Victor Payne, 19. The other air gunner, Sgt Clive Estcourt, parachuted to safety.

The air accident investigators believed that W/O Paul may have panicked in bumpy flying conditions and that his previous accident on Dartmoor may have unnerved him. Landing lights reflecting on cloud may also have led W/O Paul to believe his aircraft was on fire.

The inquiry also found that the pilot did not carry out the correct procedure for abandoning the aircraft and that he was attempting to crash land.

W/O Paul's fiancée, a New Zealand dental nurse, Violet Dunn, was devastated by his death. She never married and carried her fiance's memory through her life. After the war she visited the crash site at Farnham Common where she found shards of metal from his aircraft buried in the soil.

Miss Dunn eventually presented these precious mementoes along with W/O Paul's medals to his old school, Wellington College in New Zealand, and as a result she was invited to attend the 2007 ANZAC service, held in honour of W/O Paul.

This made a profound impression on her and the then 92 year-old Miss Dunn decided to gift the College in Thomas Paul's name $1 million towards the building of a new memorial hall and $500,000 as an endowment to promote education there. Miss Dunn died in March 2012 at the age of 95.

The Dartmoor crash had occurred when new first pilot Sgt Paul was at the controls of his own 207 Squadron Lancaster from RAF Bottesford, Lincolnshire, for a Sunday night cross-country flight. The exercise was curtailed because of bad weather and Sgt Paul was recalled to base. On the return, however, he descended in poor visibility, perhaps believing he was over the sea, and at 23.30hrs the Lancaster struck the slopes of the 1,591ft high Standon Hill. Four of the crew died instantly as the bomber broke up, but Sgt Paul and the wireless operator/air gunner Sgt Tom Whiteman survived.

The Home Guard found Sgt Whiteman, who had been thrown clear and was in shock, and took him to Standon Farm where he spent the night, but the injured Sgt Paul was not discovered until later. Those who died were the second pilot, Sgt Andrew Paterson, 31, the two observers, F/Sgt Richard Mellish, 21, and Sgt Charles Pankhurst, 35, and the other wireless operator/air gunner, F/Sgt Leonard Smith, 30.

The bomber did not catch fire in the crash and 67 MU gave a local farmer, George Mudge, the job of clearing the remains with tractor and trailer.

The official inquiry into the tragedy blamed Sgt Paul's inexperience for flying below cloud instead of over or around it, but no disciplinary action was taken.

The slopes of Standon Hill where the Lancaster crashed

DATE:	23 JUNE 1942
LOCATION/AREA:	NEAR HARROWBEER AIRFIELD
AIRCRAFT TYPE:	NORTH AMERICAN MUSTANG MKI
SERIAL NO:	AG573
SQD/UNIT:	16 SQD / CODE UG / 36 WING SOUTHERN COMMAND
BASE:	WESTONZOYLAND, SOMERSET
TIME OF CRASH:	14.45HRS
CREW:	W/CDR P. W. STANSFIELD
PURPOSE OF FLIGHT:	ARTILLERY SPOTTING
CAUSE OF CRASH:	ENGINE FAULT

NOTES:

While attempting to land at Harrowbeer, the pilot had to overshoot, but when the throttle was pushed forward no power was gained. The aircraft stalled from 20ft and crashed. W/Cdr Stansfield was injured, but not seriously.

W/Cdr P. W. Stansfield had a lucky escape

W/Cdr Stansfield's personal North American Mustang (above)

The Mustang (below) lies wrecked with its back broken

POTATO FIELD MUSTANG

A missing spring in the engine of an almost new fighter nearly cost the life of a top pilot when his North American Mustang crashed into a potato field.

RAF Weston Zoyland in Somerset was home in 1942 to 16 Squadron, part of the 36 Wing of Southern Command. It carried out offensive patrols and reconnaissance, but was also an Army co-operation squadron. For a short spell in August 1940, the squadron, then flying Westland Lysanders, was based at Okehampton (Folly Gate).

On 23 June 1942, W/Cdr P. W. Stansfield was the squadron commander. He had logged 1,202 flying hours – 22 in Mustangs – and was in the air over Dartmoor that Tuesday afternoon artillery spotting for the Army gunners during a firing exercise.

He had taken off at 14.20hrs and after 25 minutes flying over the ranges, W/Cdr Stansfield turned Mustang MKI AG573 towards the airfield at Harrowbeer, situated on the edge of the Dartmoor village of Yelverton, where he would refuel.

However, while attempting to land, W/Cdr Stansfield realised his approach was wrong and he would have to overshoot the runway. Pushing the throttle forward and raising the flaps and undercarriage to go round again, he found he could not obtain enough power and about 20ft above the ground and now a mile from the end of the runway, the Mustang stalled and crashed to the ground.

The fuselage snapped just behind the cockpit and part of the aircraft caught fire. W/Cdr Stansfield was lucky to escape with only slight injuries. He had taken over the squadron from W/Cdr Richard Hancock who died in a crash mentioned earlier in this book.

Air crash investigators came down from Farnborough and discovered that the Allison engine of W/Cdr Stansfield's aircraft was missing a spring on the accelerator pump and any sudden opening of the throttle caused the carburettor to malfunction.

As the aircraft was only six months old, having been crated from the USA to Speke, Liverpool, where it was assembled, it was assumed that the vital spring had been left out by mistake on the assembly line in the United States.

The remains of the aircraft were taken away for scrap by 67 Maintenance Unit.

W/Cdr Stansfield survived the war and in 1949 was Group Captain at RAF Marham, Norfolk. He earned a DFC and CBE.

DATE:	16 AUGUST 1942
LOCATION/AREA:	HAMEL DOWN
AIRCRAFT TYPE:	SUPERMARINE SPITFIRE MKI
SERIAL NO:	P9468
SQD/UNIT:	53 OTU / CODE QG / 81 GROUP
BASE:	LLANDOW, SOUTH WALES
TIME OF CRASH:	DAYTIME
CREW:	SGT KENNETH SPENCER HARVEY
PURPOSE OF FLIGHT:	TRAINING FLIGHT
CAUSE OF CRASH:	ENGINE FAULT/PILOT ERROR

NOTES:

The pilot disobeyed an order to keep within sight of the base and over Hamel Down had to bale out when the engine overheated.

The heather clad crash site of Sgt Kenneth Harvey's Spitfire. The post is the remains of one of the hundreds of anti-glider poles erected during the fear of invasion

RED CARD PILOT

A young pilot received a "red mark" in his log book after crashing a Battle of Britain Spitfire near Two Barrows on Hamel Down.

Sgt Kenneth Harvey had disobeyed an order and been forced to bale out when the engine of his Spitfire cut out over Widecombe.

On 16 August 1942 he had taken off in Spitfire P9468, of B Flight, 53 Operational Training Unit, for a Sunday training flight. His orders were to keep within sight of his South Wales base at RAF Llandow. Instead Sgt Harvey, with 42 hours on Spitfires, flew over the Bristol Channel, Exmoor and Dartmoor.

His temperature gauge went into the red near Widecombe and the engine cut out. Sgt Harvey turned the Spitfire upside down and took to his parachute. As he floated down, he could see his aircraft exploding on the hillside which dominates Widecombe.

He must also have been wondering what he was in for when he returned to his Glamorgan OTU. Harvey received a "red mark" - an endorsement in his log book - and was given an ear-bashing for flying more than 60 miles away from his base.

Kenneth Day and his wife Dorothy, who were staying at Powder Mills Farm during a week's holiday, happened to be walking up the shoulder of Bellever Tor at the time and he wrote later in his book Days on Dartmoor: "...and we noticed away towards Widecombe a tall column of black smoke ascending into the still air as from a factory chimney. We afterwards found that it was from a crashed plane on the ridge of Hameldon."

Many years ago I was given some parts from this Spitfire on which Westland stamps were evident, showing that they were from a repair carried out on the aircraft in 1940 after its Battle of Britain pilot Sgt Alan Harker had done a wheels-up landing at his 234 Squadron base at St Eval in Cornwall. The 24 year-old Harker later recalled that he could hear the control tower shouting to him over the radio to lower his undercarriage, but he was just too exhausted to obey. He earned a reprimand for his carelessness.

The damage was repairable which is how the aircraft came to be used at RAF Llandow for training.

During the Battle of Britain, Harker shot down eight enemy aircraft and was awarded the Distinguished Flying Medal. He survived the war and died in 1996.

Harvey was a warrant officer training others to fly Spitfires at 61 OTU when on 22 March 1946, the Spitfire XVI TW183 he was flying stalled in the circuit at RAF Keevil and crashed killing him. He was 23.

DATE:	21 AUGUST 1942
LOCATION/AREA:	GIBHILL WOOD, CORNWOOD
AIRCRAFT TYPE:	SHORT STIRLING
SERIAL NO:	R9329
SQD/UNIT:	149 SQD / CODE OJ/ 3 GROUP
BASE:	LAKENHEATH, SUFFOLK
TIME OF CRASH:	03.25HRS
CREW:	SGT G.ROBERTSON SGT P.JENKINS SGT D.HARRIS SGT D.SIMPSON SGT F.CLARKE SGT C.BOND SGT L.NICHOLSON
PURPOSE OF FLIGHT:	MINE LAYING OFF FRENCH COAST
CAUSE OF CRASH:	FLAK DAMAGE

NOTES:

The Stirling was hit by flak and flew home at a low level. It had a homing for Exeter, which was used by damaged bombers on the way back from targets on the west coast of France. It crashed into a wooded hillside and all the crew were killed.

This Stirling was built by Short Brothers and Harland and Wolff and had only flown 153hrs 45mins. The four engines were salvaged and used again after repair.

There is a memorial stone at the crash site. Also look for the two carved crosses on a tree trunk.

MYSTERY OF THE GIBHILL STIRLING

German flak or friendly fire? We will never know for certain why a giant English bomber, returning from a minelaying mission off the French coast, crashed into a wood on the edge of Dartmoor, killing all seven men on board.

The RAF flying accident report for the crash of Stirling R9329 says that it was "probably damaged" by ground defences during the operation, but the family of one of the crew believe that it was the anti-aircraft gunners protecting Plymouth who fatally damaged the bomber.

Stirling V for Victor had taken off from 149 Squadron's base at Lakenheath, Suffolk, at 20.45hrs on Thursday 20 August 1942 to lay mines off the Gironde estuary, near Bordeaux.

It was an experienced crew skippered by 25 year-old Sgt Geoffrey Robertson and they were on their 12th operation together having already taken part in many raids deep into Germany.

Robertson was highly thought of and was, in fact, promoted to pilot officer, but this was confirmed only after he was killed.

Those who died with him at 03.25hrs the following day when the Stirling struck the tops of trees in Gibhill Wood at Cornwood and crashed were flight engineer

The crash site of the Stirling at Gibhill, near Cornwood

89

Sgt Peter Jenkins, 22; observer Sgt Dudley Harris, 20; wireless operator Sgt Dennis Simpson, 26; forward turret gunner Sgt Lawrence Nicholson, 21; mid upper turret gunner Sgt Frank Clarke, 25, and rear turret gunner Sgt Cecil Bond, 19.

It is the family of Sgt Nicholson who believe there is a basis for believing the Plymouth gunners brought down the bomber and not the Germans.

David Nicholson, the brother of Sgt Nicholson, discovered during his own investigation into the crash that crews returning from south west France would use Land's End lighthouse as a marker and fly to the right of it. He thinks that in the bad weather the crew mistook the Lizard lighthouse for the one at Land's End and

One of the two crosses carved on the trunk of a large beech at the crash site

flying to the right of it took them over Plymouth where anti-aircraft defences opened fire on them.

The granite memorial dedicated in 2011

The flying accident report states that the aircraft flew into high ground and caught fire after returning from its mission over France where "it was heavily engaged by ground defences and probably damaged. As return would be made at low height it would appear that allowance was not made for the rising ground."

This Stirling had only flown 153hrs 45mins and the fire could not have reached the engines because they were used again after repair at a maintenance unit.

The two crosses carved on the trunk of a large beech tree at the crash site may have been done by a member of the salvage team when the wreckage was being cleared.

A Stirling Mk III, of 149 Squadron, pictured in March 1943 (Shorts)

In 2009 four local men, Ian Stone, Peter Sandover, Gordon Fowell and Alan Graham, began planning a more permanent memorial to the men of Stirling R9329 and in 2011 a granite pillar was unveiled by David Richardson, a nephew of crew member Sgt Nicholson, during a service of dedication.

Parts from the Stirling

DATE:	6 OCTOBER 1942
LOCATION/AREA:	ERME PITS HILL
AIRCRAFT TYPE:	VICKERS WELLINGTON MK3
SERIAL NO:	BK281
SQD/UNIT:	142 SQD / CODE QT / 1 GROUP
BASE:	GRIMSBY, LINCOLNSHIRE
TIME OF CRASH:	01.30HRS
CREW:	F/O GEORGE EDGETT (RCAF) SGT EDWARD BASTOW SGT JAMES BENNIE SGT RENE PARTINGTON F/SGT KENNETH NICHOLLS
PURPOSE OF FLIGHT:	RAID ON AACHEN, GERMANY
CAUSE OF CRASH:	BAD WEATHER
NOTES: F/Sgt Nicholls was the sole survivor when the Wellington crashed on a hill near Erme Pits, which are old tin mining works.	

Erme Pits, old tin mining works, near the crash site

FARMER'S SHOCK FIND

Dartmoor farmer Will Legassick went out early to check on his sheep – and found a crashed bomber.

Four of the crew dead were dead, but the navigator, F/Sgt Kenneth Nicholls, had survived the crash but was badly injured and Mr Legassick went off to raise the alarm.

Unbeknown to Mr Legassick, 142 Squadron at Grimsby were aware by 06.00hrs on Tuesday 6 October 1942 that one of their aircraft was missing after a raid the previous night on the German city of Aachen.

They knew that Vickers Wellington BK281 had returned to England and had probably crashed somewhere so they asked air-sea rescue specialists 276 Squadron at RAF Harrowbeer to try to find it.

At 06.10hrs, a Lysander of B flight, piloted by Canadian P/O Clarence Emberg DFC, with Sgt Kyle as observer, took off to search and at 08.15hrs they located the wreck despite the moor being shrouded in mist.

While Mr Legassick, a serving special constable, was telling his colleagues at Yelverton Police Station about his find, Defiant AA351 took off from Harrowbeer to locate the crash with information supplied by P/O Emberg. However, they could not find the missing Wellington despite making three attempts.

On landing, the Defiant pilot, S/Ldr Fisher and his two crew members, F/O Ernst and P/O Brooks, set off on foot to search the area and, after a long walk, they finally located the wreck and were able to carry the injured F/Sgt Nicholls to a waiting ambulance.

The next day, Mr Legassick, of Colleytown Farm, Sheepstor, led a police and RAF rescue team to the site to recover the bodies.

Killed in the crash was the pilot, F/O George Edgett, 28, a newcomer to the crew, who was flying only his second mission with them after joining the squadron the previous month. He was a member of the Royal Canadian Air Force and it is just possible that this was the reason why his fellow Canadian, P/O Emberg, took on the original flight to locate the crashed Wellington.

Also killed were Sgt Edward Bastow, the wireless operator/air gunner; Sgt James Bennie, the bomb aimer and Sgt Rene Partington, air gunner. With F/Sgt Nicholls, they had all joined the squadron in May.

Sgt Partington, who was 20, was the son of John and Madeleine Partington,

Killed on only his second mission: the gravestone of F/O George Edgett

who lived in Buenos Aires. They also lost another son, Sgt John Partington, who was killed on 9 June 1941 when the Wellington in which he was second pilot came down in the North Sea. He was 20 years old. The brothers had left Argentina in 1939, before hostilities began, to play their part in defeating the enemy.

The weather was already deteriorating when BK281 and the other Wellingtons took off for their mission and over Germany severe thunderstorms made finding the target difficult. Some aircraft were said to have dropped their bombs by mistake on a Dutch town.

Bad weather hampered the Wellingtons on the return flight too and at 01.30hrs BK281 crashed near Broad Rock about 400m away from Erme Head.

Broad Rock (1,480ft) marks the meeting point of the forest of Dartmoor, parish and manor boundaries as well as marking the Jobbers' Path, an ancient trans-Dartmoor wool route.

When the RAF recovery team began clearing the wreckage they found that the heavy crawler kept breaking through the surface of the peat and the operation became a lengthy one. The route off the moor was via the Eylesbarrow tin mine track to the tarmac road at what is now known as the scout hut.

DATE:	30 OCTOBER 1942
LOCATION/AREA:	FULLAMOOR FARM, NR PLASTER DOWN
AIRCRAFT TYPE:	CONSOLIDATED B24 LIBERATOR IIIA
SERIAL NO:	FK242
SQD/UNIT:	224 SQD / CODE XB
BASE:	BEAULIEU, HAMPSHIRE
TIME OF CRASH:	20.00HRS
CREW:	F/O GAVIN SELLAR P/O WILLIAM MARTIN SGT HARRY DAWE F/O VICTOR CROWTHER (RNZAF) SGT WILLIAM FRASER P/O WILLIAM CRUICKSHANKS SGT DENNIS PASS
PURPOSE OF FLIGHT:	CONVOY ESCORT DUTY
CAUSE OF CRASH:	BAD WEATHER AND MAY HAVE HIT BARRAGE BALLOON

NOTES:

Sgt Dennis Pass, aged 20, was the only survivor and did not remember the aircraft ever hitting a barrage balloon. He visited the site after the war. He died in February 1992, aged 92.

There is a small memorial plaque at the crash site, but this gives the wrong date for the crash.

This crash site is on private land, without public access.

BARRAGE BALLOON PUZZLE

The official records state that a B24 Liberator crashed into a field on Dartmoor after hitting a barrage balloon over Plymouth and yet the only survivor of the seven man crew could not recall the bomber ever striking a barrage balloon when he made a return visit to the crash site.

Rear turret gunner Sgt Dennis Pass was pulled out of the burning wreckage of Liberator FK242, which was lost in darkness and low cloud after returning from a submarine hunting patrol in the Bay of Biscay on Friday 30 October 1942.

The co-pilot, 27 year-old Sgt Harry Dawe, also survived the crash at Fullamoor Farm, but he died in the same ambulance as his gunner while on the way to Tavistock Hospital.

Those killed outright in the crash were the pilot, F/O Gavin Sellar, 21; the flight engineer, Sgt William Fraser, 24; the observer, F/O Victor Crowther, 24, of the RNZAF, and the two wireless operators/air gunners, P/O William Cruickshanks and P/O William Martin, 26. Crowther, Fraser and Martin are buried at Buckland Monachorum, not that far from the crash site; Cruickshanks is buried at Tynemouth (Preston) Cemetery, Northumberland; Dawe at Wallasey Cemetery, Cheshire and Sellar rests at Bournemouth Crematorium.

The Mark 3 Liberator had taken off from its 224 Squadron base at Beaulieu in Hampshire in search of the U-boats that infested the Bay of Biscay. The crew were all new to each other and had been crewed up just for this patrol.

No enemy submarines were encountered and on the return trip the weather deteriorated badly and they lost their bearings. We know this because Sgt Pass recalled the bomber's final hours when he returned in 1994 to Fullamoor Farm.

The retired photographer said the crew saw what they thought was the landing lights of an airfield and attempted to land only to find it was the water at the flying boat base at RAF Mount Batten on the edge of Plymouth Sound.

The B24 Liberator: the scene over Plymouth (Author's interpretation)

They climbed away searching for the airfield at Roborough and he could not recall the aircraft hitting a barrage balloon.

Surely this would have been something all the crew would have been aware of had it happened.

He did remember the two pilots suspecting the altimeter was faulty and shortly after that the B24 ploughed into the ground and skidded into a wall surrounding the field. Mr Pass remembered the aircraft hitting the ground but he then lost consciousness.

The Liberator crashed into this field wall where the gateway now stands

At Higher Pennington farm across the valley, 16 year-old William Doidge was in the house when, at about 7pm, he heard "a whoosh followed a few seconds later by a bang."

His father, also William, came running in from the yard to say a plane had crashed over near Yelverton. The two of them, plus men and boys from nearby cottages, ran up the hill towards the flames and smoke and came across the RAF fire engine from Harrowbeer stuck on a steep grass bank. They all pushed it up the hill.

The RAF men kept them away from the blazing aircraft, but they saw two men pulled from the wreckage and put in an ambulance. This was Sgt Pass and Sgt Dawe. At the RAF court of inquiry which followed the crash, it was noted that the pilot had only four hours night flying on B24s.

The gap in the field wall made by the bomber was turned into a gateway and on the right hand pillar is a plaque which reads: "This gate has filled the gap made by Liberator FK242 crashing on 31st October 1942 having been on anti-submarine duties over the Bay of Biscay.

"This plaque commemorates the gallant airmen who lost their lives in the crash. There was one survivor." The plaque is dated 31 October 1942 although the crash actually happened the day before.

The man behind the memorial was a retired Royal Navy Lieutenant Commander dental surgeon who was a close friend of the pilot, F/O Sellar, and they had attended the same school.

A small ceremony and dedication service took place which was attended by Mr Pass and his wife.

DATE:	2 NOVEMBER 1942
LOCATION/AREA:	YELVERTON VILLAGE
AIRCRAFT TYPE:	HAWKER HURRICANE MK IIB
SERIAL NO:	BP301
SQD/UNIT:	175 SQD / CODE HH
BASE:	HARROWBEER
TIME OF CRASH:	AFTERNOON
CREW:	F/O DONALD ROBERTSON (RCAF)
PURPOSE OF FLIGHT:	CONVOY EXERCISE
CAUSE OF CRASH:	BAD WEATHER/ENGINE

NOTES:

F/O Robertson, who was 23 years-old, could not gain height after taking off. When caught in a searchlight beam he took evasive action, but stalled and spun into the ground and was killed.

The squadron's operations record book for 6.11.42 states: "Today we buried Robbie with full honours at Buckland. It was an impressive funeral, a fitting homage to a gallant soul."

F/O Robertson came from Edmonton, Canada. He was just 23 years-old.

A gallant soul: the headstone of F/O Donald Robertson

DATE:	9 NOVEMBER 1942
LOCATION/AREA:	HARROWBEER
AIRCRAFT TYPE:	BOULTON PAUL DEFIANT
SERIAL NO:	N3444
SQD/UNIT:	NO.2 DELIVERY FLIGHT / CODE AQ
BASE:	HONEYBOURNE, WORCS
TIME OF CRASH:	15.15HRS
CREW:	SGT SYDNEY ARTHUR WATKINS SGT DOUGLAS SMALL
PURPOSE OF FLIGHT:	DELIVERY FLIGHT TO 276 SQD
CAUSE OF CRASH:	ENGINE FAULT

NOTES: When flying over the airfield the engine cut out and the pilot, Sgt Watkins, tried to turn back towards the runway. However, because of the lack of flying speed the aircraft plunged into the ground and both crewmen were killed.

A Boulton Paul Defiant (Boulton Paul)

DATE:	2 DECEMBER 1942
LOCATION/AREA:	WHITE TOR, PETER TAVY
AIRCRAFT TYPE:	SUPERMARINE SPITFIRE MK VB
SERIAL NO:	EP749
SQD/UNIT:	19 SQD / CODE QV
BASE:	PERRANPORTH
TIME OF CRASH:	DAYTIME
CREW:	P/O W.M.CIECHANOWSKI (POL)
PURPOSE OF FLIGHT:	NAVIGATION EXERCISE
CAUSE OF CRASH:	BAD WEATHER

NOTES: The Polish pilot, P/O Wladyslaw Ciechanowski, had taken off from his Cornwall base for a navigation exercise and while over Dartmoor the weather closed in. It is thought that the pilot came down below cloud to try to pinpoint his position and hit the high ground near White Tor. The aircraft was found the next day with the pilot dead in the wreckage. He is buried at Exeter Higher Cemetery.

The grave of P/O W.M.M. Ciechanowski at Exeter Higher Cemetery

DATE:	18 JANUARY 1943
LOCATION/AREA:	YELLAND FARM, Nr. OKEHAMPTON
AIRCRAFT TYPE:	FAIREY FULMAR
SERIAL NO:	X8812
SQD/UNIT:	781 SQD FAA / CODE J
BASE:	LEE-ON-THE-SOLENT
TIME OF CRASH:	DAYTIME
CREW:	LT RANDOLPH TRAFFORD AA4 JOHN TYRRELL
PURPOSE OF FLIGHT:	FERRY FLIGHT TO RNAS FORD, W. SUSSEX
CAUSE OF CRASH:	BAD WEATHER

NOTES: This aircraft had been on the carrier HMS Victorious in June 1942 and was then based on the carrier HMS Indomitable when one of its wings was damaged in an attack by enemy fighters on 12 August 1942 while it was being flown by Lt L. J. Wallace.

For this ferry flight to RNAS Ford in West Sussex, Lt Trafford had taken off from St Merryn, but just before Okehampton, the aircraft struck high ground in poor visibility. Both crewmen were killed.

Many years ago, the engine was recovered. There is nothing to see there now and the crash site is on private land.

The slimline Fairey Fulmar

DATE:	4 FEBRUARY 1943
LOCATION/AREA:	MEAVY, NEAR YELVERTON
AIRCRAFT TYPE:	HAWKER TYPHOON MK 1B
SERIAL NO:	DN510
SQD/UNIT:	193 SQD / CODE DP / 10 GROUP
BASE:	HARROWBEER
TIME OF CRASH:	MORNING
CREW:	P/O WILL KILPATRICK
PURPOSE OF FLIGHT:	LOCAL PRACTICE FLIGHT
CAUSE OF CRASH:	STRUCTURAL FAILURE

NOTES: The tail of the Typhoon broke off when in a dive at 400mph. P/O "Killy" Kilpatrick was almost thrown out when the hood came off and momentarily lost consciousness. He eventually baled out. He was the only pilot to survive such a tail failure and continued flying until the end of the war.

The Typhoon's tail broke off in a dive (Author's interpretation)

Talk about the luck of the Irish! P/O Will "Killy" Kilpatrick was the only survivor of the 13 Hawker Typhoon pilots whose aircraft crashed between 1942 and 1943 as a result of structural failure of the tail units.

He also survived another Typhoon crash during the battle of Mortain in 1944 when, after

1993, we meet again: P/O Killy Kilpatrick (left) with one of the men who helped him after his crash, Ted Palmer. (Tavistock Times)

being taken prisoner, he persuaded his six-strong German escort to defect and then managed to capture 24 well-armed Austrians.

No wonder his commanding officer ordered the bar to be kept open when the popular Killy returned to his squadron a few days later having handed over his 30 prisoners to the Free French.

The six-ton Typhoon was the first RAF fighter capable of speeds in excess of 400mph in level flight, but the 2,250hp Napier Sabre engine brought with it various problems, such as pulling to the right when taxiing and a massive swing as the tail wheel came off the ground. The most infamous problem of all, though, was tail-off failure.

Harrowbeer was home to 193 Squadron of Typhoons, but the squadron was not operational when P/O Kilpatrick took off on 4 February 1943 for a practice flight in MN510, a new aircraft which had just been delivered to the squadron.

He was at 30,000ft over Dartmoor and the view was so good that he put his harness on half release and raised his seat to see better. This probably saved his life.

He offered to intercept when he overheard Exeter control over his radio announce a possible incoming raid, but he was ordered to land as he was non-operational.

He turned back towards Harrowbeer, but in a diving turn at 27,000ft the tail snapped off and the Typhoon went into a sudden dive. His head broke through the Perspex canopy and he was being strangled by his oxygen tube and radio wires and lost consciousness.

The aircraft descended to about 6,000ft, which released the pressure on the harness. P/O Kilpatrick regained consciousness and threw himself out and his parachute opened itself.

The Typhoon spun into the ground near Meavy and the pilot came down about a mile away. Farm workers raced to his aid and an ambulance with doctor aboard soon arrived from Harrowbeer. He was taken to Tavistock Hospital where he made a full recovery.

The farm workers were told by RAF intelligence officers that he had been shot down as they did not want anyone to find out about the structural weakness of the Typhoon tail.

The fault was kept secret until a repair modification was put in place, which comprised a strap bolted around the tail joint. After this, the Typhoon had fewer failures.

P/O Kilpatrick was later asked to go to the Hawker factory to be interviewed by test pilots. In January 1945, he was awarded the DSO.

In August 1993, Killy returned to Devon to meet one of the farm workers, Ted Palmer, who had helped him and was presented with a piece of the Perspex from his canopy by a group who had dug up parts of his Typhoon.

The story of how P/O Kilpatrick captured 30 enemy soldiers after being shot down by flak in France is worth recounting. He hid underneath one of the tanks he had been trying to blow up, but was spotted and arrested. He and a downed American P-47 pilot, Emil Birza, were given a six man escort of Germans, but the Irishman with the gift of the gab persuaded them they would be better off if they defected, which they agreed to do.

Later they were approached by 24 heavily- armed troops who turned out to be Austrians. A big Allied raid began and P/O Kilpatrick pointed out to the Austrians that their shiny tunic buttons would easily be seen by the aircraft.

The Austrians dropped their weapons and ran to a nearby barn to hide. P/O Kilpatrick and his American pal picked up two rifles and promptly captured the Austrians.

All 30 prisoners were later handed over to the Free French and the smiling Irishman headed home to Blighty and the bar.

DATE:	15 FEBRUARY 1943
LOCATION/AREA:	KING TOR HALT
AIRCRAFT TYPE:	HAWKER TYPHOON
SERIAL NO:	DN310
SQD/UNIT:	193 SQD /CODE DP/ 10 GROUP
BASE:	HARROWBEER
TIME OF CRASH:	09.40HRS
CREW:	F/O RICHARD DUNSMUIR
PURPOSE OF FLIGHT:	LOW ALTITUDE FORMATION FLYING
CAUSE OF CRASH:	BAD WEATHER

NOTES:

While flying over King Tor, the aircraft hit an upward air current from the tor, stalled and spun into the ground. The pilot was killed.

The King Tor Halt crash site

DATE:	28 FEBRUARY 1943
LOCATION/AREA:	HARROWBEER AIRFIELD
AIRCRAFT TYPE:	H.P HALIFAX MKII
SERIAL NO:	W7906
SQD/UNIT:	35 SQD / CODE TL / 8(PFF) GROUP
BASE:	RAF GRAVELEY, CAMBRIDGE
TIME OF CRASH:	23.35HRS
CREW:	ACTING S/LDR D.DEAN DFC SGT D.R.CRAIG P/O D.P.D.ARCHER P/O A.E.R.BEXTON P/O A.R.BALL SGT J.GRIFFIN
PURPOSE OF FLIGHT:	OPERATION TO ST NAZAIRE
CAUSE OF CRASH:	ENGINE FAILURE

NOTES: The pilot pressed home the attack on three engines and on the return another engine failed. The crew were getting ready to ditch when the searchlights of Plymouth were seen. Harrowbeer was contacted for a landing and the bomber touched down halfway along the 11,000ft runway and ran off the end and across the road. The crew escaped injury.

A 35 Squadron Halifax

All right, so this tale does not feature an aircraft written off, but the drama did end at a Dartmoor airfield and the story is too good to leave out.

It was hardly surprisingly that Acting Squadron Leader Donald Dean had been given the sobriquet "Dixie" in the RAF after the famous Everton and England footballer "Dixie" Dean.

However, S/Ldr Dean's climb to the top, which took in the elite Pathfinder force after stints with 35 and 77 Squadrons, almost ended in 1941. He was the second pilot of a H.P Whitley returning from a bombing raid on Bremen in the early hours of 28 July when an engine failed over the Friesian Islands and the crew had to ditch. They spent three days in a small dinghy before being rescued by two motor gun-boats.

It was during his second tour of operations that the now Acting Squadron Leader almost found himself in a dinghy once more. He had taken off from 35 Squadron's Cambridgeshire base at RAF Graveley on 28 February 1943 to attack the German-occupied naval base at St Nazaire. His crew was made up of Sgt D. R. Craig, P/O D. P. D. Archer, P/O A. E. R. Bexton, P/O A. R. Ball and Sgt J. Griffin.

They were halfway across the channel when the port outer engine failed, but S/Ldr Dean feathered the engine and pressed on to complete his bombing run during which the anti-aircraft fire was heavy.

After leaving the target area, the starboard inner engine failed and S/Ldr Dean ordered the crew to ditching stations, ascended to 3,000ft and set course for Exeter. Approaching the coast, heavy cloud was encountered, but searchlights were seen above the cloud tops and the pilot realised he was close to Plymouth.

Dropping down through the clouds, an airfield was seen but no indication for the direction of landing was observed and neither were the crew able to establish air to ground communications.

The airfield turned out to be Harrowbeer and S/Ldr Dean managed to put down the Halifax halfway along the 11,000ft runway. The Halifax ran off the end of the runway and across the road, some of the engines breaking off. All the crew, though, escaped injury.

S/Ldr Dean was awarded a bar to his DFC for fulfilling his mission "with commendable courage and skill." The Halifax was actually repaired, but was lost over St Nazaire later in the year.

Dean went on to have a glittering career in the RAF and was also awarded the DSO in 1944 and was mentioned in Despatches. He also held the US Silver Star but this does not appear to have been actually presented to him. This genius of a pilot died in May 1997.

DATE;	9 MARCH 1943
LOCATION/AREA:	HARROWBEER AIRFIELD
AIRCRAFT TYPE:	SUPERMARINE SPITFIRE VB
SERIAL NO:	AD243
SQD/UNIT:	302 SQD
BASE:	HUTTON CRANSWICK, YORKSHIRE
TIME OF CRASH:	NIGHT
CREW:	UNKNOWN
PURPOSE OF FLIGHT:	NIGHT FLYING PRACTICE
CAUSE OF CRASH:	HIT FENCE ON LANDING

NOTES:

The only details available are that the pilot was slightly injured, but the aircraft was a write off after hitting a fence. As this was a Polish squadron, it is quite likely that the pilot involved was Polish.

Harrowbeer airfield just after the war. The church can be seen in the lower middle of the picture (Philip Jenkinson)

DATE:	18 MAY 1943
LOCATION/AREA:	HARROWBEER AIRFIELD
AIRCRAFT TYPE:	BOULTON PAUL DEFIANT MKI
SERIAL NO:	AA569
SQD/UNIT:	286 SQD (AAC) / CODE NW
BASE:	WESTON-SUPER-MARE, ON DETACHMENT TO HARROWBEER
TIME OF CRASH:	13.29 HRS
CREW:	F/SGT I. V. PETERS
PURPOSE OF FLIGHT:	ARMY CO-OPERATION
CAUSE OF CRASH:	PILOT ERROR

NOTES: Three men were killed and six injured during the Defiant's failed take-off from the Dartmoor airfield. The Defiant swung badly and careered into an Army lorry waiting at the side of the runway to cross. The lorry was packed with men of the 468 Battery, 29 (Kent) Searchlight Regiment, who had come up from Liskeard to attend an aircraft recognition training day at the airfield and were on their way back to Cornwall.

Three of them were killed. They were Lance Bombardier William George Longhurst, 22, and Gunners R.V.S. Massey and R. Brittain. The injured men were Sgt Munn and Gunners Dubber, Durant, Elliott, Rogers and Allison.

The pilot of the Defiant, F/Sgt Peters, was also injured. Longhurst is buried at St. Stephens By Saltash Churchyard, Cornwall.

Boulton Paul Defiant
(Boulton Paul)

DATE:	1 JUNE 1943
LOCATION/AREA:	KITTY TOR
AIRCRAFT TYPE:	VICKERS WELLINGTON
SERIAL NO:	MP597
SQD/UNIT:	3 OADU / CODE UNKNOWN
BASE:	HURN, DORSET
TIME OF CRASH:	06.30HRS
CREW:	F/O G.S.WATTERSON SGT J. DIXON SGT G.V.COLLIS SGT W.H.SIMPSON P/O P.J.EVANS SGT A.MOONEY
PURPOSE OF FLIGHT:	DELIVERY FLIGHT TO N. AFRICA VIA GIBRALTAR
CAUSE OF CRASH:	BAD WEATHER

NOTES: This aircraft was on the first stage of its flight when in bad weather it hit high ground near Kitty Tor. The second pilot, Sgt John Dixon, 22, was killed and the wireless operator, Sgt Collis, severely injured. F/O Watterson went off in search of help and two and a half hours later stumbled into Meldon Quarry. About 100 men took part in the successful rescue.

Sgt Dixon is buried in Shildon (St. John) Churchyard, Durham.

Looking towards Meldon Quarry processing plant. The quarry is no longer operational.

These exquisite paintings appear on a citation presented to Meldon Quarry to honour the heroic efforts of their quarrymen in the rescue of the crew of a crashed bomber.

MELDON'S BRAVE SAVE THE DAY

An injured pilot staggered into fog shrouded Meldon Quarry and sparked arguably the most dramatic rescue in Dartmoor's history.

Up to 100 men searched an area of 10 square miles in appalling weather to rescue the injured crew of a crashed Wellington bomber.

The co-pilot was killed in the crash and a local doctor, who treated the injured men, said the rest of the crew owed their lives to the quarrymen who had downed tools to find them and stretchered them over difficult terrain for three and a half miles to safety.

The six man crew immediately after the crash (Author's interpretation)

Wellington MP597, of 3 Overseas Aircraft Delivery Unit, had taken off at 06.00hrs on Tuesday 1 June 1943 from RAF Hurn (now Bournemouth airport) for a delivery flight to North Africa.

The pilot was F/O George Watterson whose crew was made up of Sgt John Dixon, the co-pilot; Sgt W.H. Simpson, the navigator; Sgt G.V. Collis, the wireless operator, and the two wireless operator/air gunners, P/O P. J. Evans and Sgt A. Mooney.

The route was over Tiverton, Newquay, Scilly Isles and Bay of Biscay, landing at Gibraltar to refuel. Thirty minutes after passing over Tiverton, the aircraft turned onto a course which took it over northern Dartmoor instead of around the edge. Had they even been 20ft higher they would have cleared the high ground and been clear for Newquay, but in the mist they struck near the top of Kitty Tor (1,920ft).

Sgt Dixon was killed in the crash, Sgt Collis was seriously injured and all the other crew members had various injuries. Perhaps the injuries suffered by F/O Watterson were not as bad as the others, which is why he went off in search of help for his men.

Dr Douglas Routh, of Okehampton, was called to the quarry to treat the injured pilot. F/O Watterson told his story and wanted to help look for the crash site with the rescuers, but Dr Routh would not let him go because of his injuries.

The quarry manager, Mr F.E.L. Weaver, stopped all work at the quarry and divided his workers into several small teams to search for the downed Wellington. Carrying stretchers and other equipment they set off as the weather became increasingly bad. Nevertheless, the course of the Red-a-ven brook and West Okement river was scoured and also the high ground including Longstone Hill (1,300ft), Homerton Hill (1,290ft), Branscombe Loaf (1,750ft), Black Down (1,433ft) and Yes Tor (2,030ft).

At about 10.00hrs – just over three hours after the crash – five men checking the West Okement valley decided to work their way up to Kitty Tor and it was here that quarryman Bill Turner saw the tail of the crashed aeroplane through the mist. He called over the others who were G. Dawe, Fred Dennis, tool lad Cyril Squires and T. Lake, a worker from another quarry.

Mr Turner then returned to the quarry to fetch more help and equipment and Mr Dennis stayed with the crew to administer first aid. Eventually Dr Routh was guided up to the site by quarryman M. Cook and they gave further medical help.

The rescuers found Sgt Collis, the wireless operator, was the most severely

injured and he and the dead co-pilot were put on stretchers and taken down to waiting ambulances at the quarry. The other injured crew members, P/O Evans, Sgt Simpson and Sgt Mooney, waited for further stretchers. During all this time, there was no let-up in the mist and torrential rain.

Eventually, all the crew were stretchered down to safety and Dr Routh said later that he doubted if the injured crew would have survived had they not been rescued.

At the subsequent court of inquiry, the pilot and navigator were blamed equally for the crash, the pilot for flying at too low an altitude, and the navigator for being uncertain of his position.

George Ellson, the chief engineer of the Southern Railway, instigated and presented the citation

All the injured men made full recoveries, apart from Sgt Collis, who was medically discharged from the RAF later the same year. The rest of the crew all survived the war. F/O Watterson retired from the RAF in 1966 with the rank of wing commander.

George Ellson, the chief engineer of the Southern Railway, who owned the quarry, was so impressed by the heroic efforts of the quarrymen of Meldon that he presented the quarry manager, Mr Weaver, who had taken part in and organised the rescue, with a framed citation detailing the dramatic rescue, with the names of the stretcher bearers around the side.

This citation is written in a beautiful hand and at the top are two small exquisite paintings showing part of the rescue and a larger one of the scene which met the first rescuers, with the tail of the crashed aircraft sticking up through the mist.

The bottom of the citation is signed S. W. Weaver July 1943. This Weaver may well have been related to the quarry manager, perhaps his wife or brother, and these scenes must have been described to the artist by someone who was present.

Each of the rescuers was given a photograph of the framed citation. What a proud day it must have been for the quarry when these were presented. The quarrymen must have felt they had played a true part in helping to win the war.

The framed citation to the rescue shown by Paul Hambling,
the archivist at the Museum of Dartmoor Life, Okehampton

The framed citation hung for many years in the quarry mess, but was donated to the Museum of Dartmoor Life at Okehampton by Mr Weaver, the former quarry manager, in 1993. The museum also has two of the photographs given to the individual rescuers.

The names of the stretcher bearers on the citation are A. Baskerville, L. Bowden, C. Cooke, F. Doidge, W. Hollands, T. Knight, T. Pope, A. Piper, S. Sims, F. Dennis, L. Palmer, G. Wooldridge, R. Bickle, R. Burnham, G. Dawe, L. Fone, C. Jewell, W. Neno, D. Pellow, P. Shaddick, L. Walmesley, F. Dodd, A.Parker. The words "and others" is then added.

It is a shame that the citation is in storage and not actually on display at this excellent museum.

Kitty Tor

DATE:	28 JULY 1943
LOCATION/AREA:	HARROWBEER
AIRCRAFT TYPE:	HAWKER TYPHOON MK IB
SERIAL NO:	JP393
SQD/UNIT:	183 SQ / CODE HF
BASE:	HARROWBEER
TIME OF CRASH:	DAYTIME
CREW:	F/SGT R.N. FOSTER
PURPOSE OF FLIGHT:	LOW LEVEL SWEEP
CAUSE OF CRASH:	TYRE FAILURE

NOTES:

A tyre burst as the Typhoon was taking off and F/Sgt Foster raised the undercarriage to stop and belly-flopped onto the runway. He was congratulated for keeping his head and acting correctly to avoid damage to buildings.

F/O Foster, 21, was taking part in a six aircraft mission over Kerlin Bastard Airfield in France on 31 January 1944 when he was shot down by anti-aircraft fire. His Typhoon was hit in the starboard wing petrol tank and although he was seen to jettison his hood, the aircraft exploded before he could bale out. He is buried at Guidel Communal Cemetery in France.

F/O Richard Foster
(Aircrew Remembered and
family of Gillian Cornwall)

DATE:	7 JULY 1943
LOCATION/AREA:	NEAR HARROWBEER AIRFIELD
AIRCRAFT TYPE:	HAWKER TYPHOON IB
SERIAL NO:	JP404
SQD/UNIT:	183 SQD/ CODE HF
BASE:	HARROWBEER
TIME OF CRASH:	18.15HRS
CREW:	F/O E.GOTTOWT (POL)
PURPOSE OF FLIGHT:	TRAINING FLIGHT
CAUSE OF CRASH:	UNKNOWN

NOTES:

Polish F/O Eugeniusz Gottowt, 27, died when his Typhoon plunged into the ground from 6,000ft. The pilot did not try to bale out until he had lost half of his height.

At the court of inquiry, it was stated that pilots should be shown how to jettison the car-type door and hood. Later Typhoons had bubble hoods which were easier to bale out from. This aircraft was only five days old.

F/O Gottowt had escaped another crash several days before.

F/O Eugeniusz Gottowt (Polish Institute and Sikorski Museum)

DATE:	2 OCTOBER 1943
LOCATION/AREA:	WESTERN BEACON, IVYBRIDGE
AIRCRAFT TYPE:	SUPERMARINE SPITFIRE MK VC
SERIAL NO:	AB453
SQD/UNIT:	610 SQD / CODE DW
BASE:	PERRANPORTH, CORNWALL, DETACHMENT TO BOLT HEAD, DEVON
TIME OF CRASH:	17.52HRS
CREW:	F/O S.J.SHEWELL (RCAF)
PURPOSE OF FLIGHT:	PRACTICE FORMATION AND CINE ATTACKS
CAUSE OF CRASH:	PILOT ERROR

NOTES:

While flying at between 300 and 400ft, the aircraft stalled on a tight turn and, with no height to recover, crashed and burst into flames, killing the pilot.

F/O Stanley Joseph 'Scarlet' Shewell, who came from Owen Sound, Ontario, is buried at Haycombe Cemetery, Bath. He was known as 'Scarlet' because of his red hair.

This Spitfire was named Kenya Daisy by the Kenya pyrethrum growers and the Digo Local Native Council who raised £5,000 to purchase a Spitfire. A pyrethrum is any of several forms of cultivated Eurasian chrysanthemums.

F/O Stanley Joseph "Scarlet" Shewell

DATE:	3 DECEMBER 1943
LOCATION/AREA:	STEEPERTON TOR
AIRCRAFT TYPE:	CONSOLIDATED PB4Y-1
SERIAL NO:	32014 – B13
SQD/UNIT:	VB 103 USN
BASE:	DUNKESWELL
TIME OF CRASH:	EARLY MORNING
CREW:	LT T.A.LUCAS LT J.H.ALEXANDER ENS D.B.SHEA ENS F.J.BUCKLEY AMM1 T.L.RAY ARM W.A.TGAN AMM2 R.J.O'LEARY AOM2 W.H.DAVIDSON AMM3 E.A.SHUBERT AOM2 J.B.LAUBTNGER
PURPOSE OF FLIGHT:	BOMBING TRAINING FLIGHT
CAUSE OF CRASH:	BAD WEATHER

NOTES: This was the first of four crashes in the month which would cost the lives of 33 Americans. Bad weather and possible icing of the aircraft caused the crash which killed all the crew. Tracked vehicles were used for the first time in the recovery of the wreckage.

The PB4Y-1 Berlin Express and crew that lost their lives at Steeperton Tor (Bernard Stevens)

An iconic shot of the ill-fated Berlin Express looking towards another US Navy Liberator at Dunkeswell (Bernard Stevens)

BLACK DECEMBER FOR AMERICANS

William Davidson volunteered to replace a sick air gunner on a routine instrument training flight from the submarine hunting Dunkeswell air base in mid Devon and was among the 10-man crew who died instantly when a US Navy Liberator struck Steeperton Tor.

It was the first of four crashes on the moor involving American aircraft in December 1943 costing in total the lives of 33 young servicemen.

It also resulted in an epic nine-day clear up operation in which tracked vehicles were used for the first time.

The Pilot Lt Tony Lucas
(via David Earl)

On Friday 3 December, two PB4Y-1 Liberators had taken off for a training flight which would take them over Plymouth Sound. AOM2C Davidson was in Liberator 32014 - nicknamed Berlin Express - which was piloted by Lt Tony Lucas, who had Lt James Alexander as his co-pilot.

Lt Alexander, 23, had been recommended for the Navy Cross following a mission three months before when he had beaten off the attack of six Ju-88s before safely landing his Catalina flying boat in the sea and saving his crew.

Also aboard for the training flight were Ens Donald Shea, Ens Francis Buckley,

Steeperton Tor, where the PB4Y-1 Liberator crashed

AMM1C Theodore Ray, ARM2C Wilse Tgan, AMM2C Richard O'Leary, AMM3C Eldret Shubert and AOM2C James Laubtnger.

Their aircraft was flying on instruments and in mist at the time of the crash which was heard but not seen by two Army officers who later reported that the engines seemed to be running smoothly.

The only surviving parts of this aircraft.

From the information contained in the operations record book (ORB) of the 67 Maintenance Unit, who were involved in the clear-up operation, it seems that the Liberator struck the east slope of Steeperton Tor and wreckage was strewn down the steep hillside for a distance of 600 yards. Two engines lodged halfway down, but the other two bounced across a stream at the bottom of the valley. This would be the Steeperton Brook.

It was not possible to bring RAF vehicles closer than one and a half miles and a six wheel drive vehicle had to be borrowed from the US Army detachments at Okehampton Camp. The Royal Artillery also loaned Dragons – tracked vehicles used for towing guns.

The ORB says that the engines were removed by a clee tractor – like a normal tractor but with tracked wheels – and sledge. The stream had to be bridged with railway sleepers to get the engines on the sledge.

The engines were then winched up the hillside before being sledged to the nearest track. The lighter wreckage was carried in the Dragons while propellers and undercarriage were sledged.

The Dragons were also used to pull a low loader which had been brought in to help but which bottomed in a stream.

Okehampton Fire Brigade raced to the scene and were in such a hurry that the trailer pump unit became disconnected when they went through a stream. They just left it and carried on. The whole salvage took nine days and fortunately the weather stayed favourable.

After the war, some of Davidson's original crew were among those who attended his memorial service.

DATE:	26 OCTOBER 1943
LOCATION/AREA:	HARROWBEER AIRFIELD
AIRCRAFT TYPE:	HAWKER TYPHOON IB
SERIAL NO:	JP497
SQD/UNIT:	193 SQD
BASE:	HARROWBEER
TIME OF CRASH:	UNKNOWN
CREW:	F/O JOHN ALEXANDER INGLIS
PURPOSE OF FLIGHT:	UNKNOWN
CAUSE OF CRASH	MISFIRING ENGINE, THROTTLE JAMMED AND RETRACTED UNDERCARRIAGE

NOTES: The Typhoon crashed in a forced landing and was written off. The Pilot was unhurt.

F/O Inglis, 23, always known as Jock, was killed 12 June 1944 when his Typhoon 1B MN 252 was hit by flak and crashed south east of Potigny. He is buried in St. Charles de Percy War Cemetery, Calvados.

Jock Inglis (centre) and ground crew (via Pierre Vandervelden)

In November 1943 this squadron was used to attack German V-1 rocket launch sites.

Some of the squadron's Typhoons were paid for by the Brazilian branch of the Fellowship of the Bellows, an international group set up during the war to raise funds to buy aircraft for the RAF.

DATE:	25 DECEMBER 1943
LOCATION/AREA:	TIGER'S MARSH, NORTH OF GREN TOR
AIRCRAFT TYPE:	BOEING B17-G
SERIAL NO:	44-1225507
SQD/UNIT:	517 MET SQD RAF / EIGHTH AIR FORCE
BASE:	BOVINGTON, DEPARTED CHEDDINGTON
TIME OF CRASH:	12.15HRS
CREW:	1 LT ERNEST PATTERSON 2 LT RAYMOND COATS 2 LT RICHARD NEARY T/SGT SHERWOOD RENNER T/SGT SAMUEL CRAIG S/SGT MARIO PANETTI S/SGT ALBENY BLANCHARD SGT BASIL BROWNE RAF
PURPOSE OF FLIGHT:	MET FLIGHT
CAUSE OF CRASH:	PILOT ERROR

NOTES:

The crew were asked to stay for Christmas lunch at St Eval, where they had gone for repairs to a faulty engine, but wanted to return to Cheddington. They ran into mist on the way and crashed near Gren Tor. 1 Lt Patterson, 2 Lt Coats, and Sgt Browne were the only survivors.

There are some bits of wreckage lying around at the crash site and there are two small memorial plaques. Be wary, the area can be boggy and dangerous.

The original crew of the Flying Fortress although not all of them were on the final mission. The six of them that were include pilot Ernest Patterson, standing third from left in the back row, who survived. Those killed were navigator Richard Neary, first left in the back row, and the first four in the front row, from the left, Samuel Craig, radio operator/gunner; Mario Panetti, radio operator/gunner; Sherwood Renner, engineer, and Albeny Blanchard, gunner (US Airforce)

CHRISTMAS DAY TRAGEDY

A teenage sergeant's warning that an American bomber was flying too low over Dartmoor could not prevent the B-17 from crashing on Christmas Day 1943 with the loss of five members of the crew.

Miraculously, the pilot and co-pilot survived as did the only Englishman on board, an 18-year-old RAF meteorological observer Sgt Basil Browne, whose warning helped save their lives.

The two pilots stumbled off the moor to find help thinking that their weather expert was dead.

The B-17 was on its way back to its Buckinghamshire base at Cheddington after a flight to gather weather data over the Western Approaches. The pilot, 1 Lt Ernest Patterson, had been forced to curtail the mission after about 350 miles because of an overheating engine and he had landed at St Eval in Cornwall for a new oil filter to be fitted and to refuel.

The crew had a quick nap while the work was carried out and were then asked if they wanted to stay for Christmas lunch. Sgt Browne wanted to accept, but the Americans were keen to get back to their own base to celebrate Christmas.

So Flying Fortress 44-1225507, of 517 Met Squadron, took off from St Eval at 11.30hrs and, with his job already done, young Sgt Browne borrowed a map to try out his recently acquired skills of navigation and map reading from his usual position in the nose of the aircraft. He had seen spot heights of about 1,800ft (550m) on their track near Dartmoor and noticed that they were flying at 1,200ft (370m). He pointed this out to the navigator, who was behind him, and he relayed it to the pilot who said it was okay as the visibility was good and he was using the radio altimeter.

Shortly after this, the B-17 flew into cloud and the pilot began to climb, but it was not quickly enough and the aircraft struck the top of a hill, rupturing the fuel tanks, and then flew on for approximately three-quarters of a mile on fire before crashing in Tiger's Marsh, an area of miry ground close to the infant River Lyd and near Gren Tor.

Sgt Browne was catapulted through the Perspex nose of the aircraft, knocking him unconscious and breaking his right wrist when his watch strap caught on the bomb site.

The author painted this dramatic picture of the crash after several talks with survivor Basil Browne (Author's interpretation)

1 Lt Patterson and his co-pilot, 2 Lt Raymond Coats, were able to climb quickly out of the cockpit. They believed they were the only survivors.

They staggered off the moor and reached the home of the Meadows family who lived in a little cottage below Lake Viaduct. The ruins of this cottage are still there, the chimney standing tall but now smothered by ivy.

None of the family had ever seen American uniforms and Mr Meadows was at first alarmed, thinking they could be Germans. He sent his two eldest daughters, Ivy and Mabel, running off to raise the alarm while 16-year-old Sylvia stayed with her parents. The two girls alerted Ronald Jury, who lived in a cottage the other side of the road, and he in turn went to see Reg Ellis at the nearby hamlet of Southerly. A member of the Home Guard, Ellis had a telephone and contacted the authorities.

Teenage sergeant Basil Browne, who survived after being thrown clear during the crash

Both airmen were burnt, but one more than the other and he sat outside in the cool fresh air to try to alleviate the pain of his burns. The other airman sat inside speaking with Mr Meadows. Eventually an American ambulance arrived to take them away.

Bill Heathman, who lived in one of the cottages which now forms the Bearslake Inn, was entertaining his brother-in-law Bill Ayres to Christmas lunch when he heard the news about the crashed American bomber. Heathman and Ayers were the first rescuers on the scene and found a dazed Sgt Browne wandering around near the burning bomber.

Ayres gave the sergeant his Sunday best jacket to wear as his tunic was wet and he was shivering with cold and sat him down by a rock.

"You told me you were up with the pilots and that the three of you were shot out on impact and were the only survivors. It was a pretty gruesome sight that I shall never forget," wrote Ayres in a letter to Sgt Browne after the war.

"You see the front half of the plane was across the bog. Two airmen were on the rushes nearly across and the mid gunner was still in his seat, but we could not do anything for them because they were dead.

"Clothing, maps, ammunition was everywhere and we were lucky not to have stopped one. It was going off and flying everywhere."

Sgt Browne was eventually driven away in a jeep and Ayres had to run after it to get his jacket back and return the tunic to Sgt Browne. The crew members killed in the crash were 2 Lt Richard Neary, the navigator; S/Sgt Mario Panetti, radio operator and gunner; T/Sgt Sherwood Renner, engineer; T/ Sgt Samuel Craig, radio operator and gunner, and S/Sgt Albeny Blanchard, gunner.

The names of Coats, Neary, Panetti and Browne are spelt wrongly on the brass memorial plaque which can be found at the crash site. In 2011, a stainless steel plaque also appeared at the site. This has all the American names spelt correctly but still misses the final "e" from Sgt Browne's name.

The bodies of three of the crew were returned to their families. The other two crew members who perished are buried at the US Military Cemetery in Cambridge. In the official aircraft accident report, the time of the crash is given as 12.15pm. It says the aircraft entered mist which was prevalent over the moors.

It goes on: "The aircraft skimmed over the first hill, which is 1,430ft above sea level, and found low cloud hanging in valley beyond. Pilot started climbing immediately and went on instruments as he was then in the clouds. Aircraft was not climbing rapidly enough and hit the top of the next hill, which is 1,750ft above sea level. The aircraft bounced along approximately three-quarters of a mile. Bomb bay gas tanks were apparently split open and fire started almost immediately.

"Two of the crew were thrown clear and the pilot and co-pilot got out when the aircraft came to rest. Aircraft was totally destroyed by crash and ensuing fire."

The report added: "The co-pilot reported altimeter reading of 2,300ft at the time of the crash. This could not be checked as aircraft was destroyed."

A photograph taken a few days after the crash by the US Airforce, shows investigators looking at the wreckage. (US Airforce)

The pilot, co-pilot and Sgt Browne made full recoveries, but that was not the end of the story.

While at the crash site, Bill Heathman had picked up a silver cigarette case and when he returned home he gave it to his seven year-old son, Roy. It had BB engraved on it plus the name B Browne and an obscure Rotherham address.

Parts from the B17, Basil Browne's watch in centre.

In middle age, Roy Heathman ran a local garage and when a couple paid for their petrol by cheque with the name Rotherham on it, Roy remembered the cigarette case and told them the story of how he obtained it. The couple said they knew a family called Browne – and amazingly it turned out to be former Met observer Basil Browne. He and Roy Heathman were later able to talk on the telephone about that day.

Fast forward to 1983 and a Mr Hatcher from Exeter was out near the crash site and found a watch. He thought no more about it until 11 years later when he heard the author of this book, Graham Lewis, being interviewed on the radio about another crash.

Mr Hatcher contacted me, gave me the watch he had found and told me there might be a story behind it. After six weeks of investigative work, I discovered that the owner of the watch was none other than ex sergeant Basil Browne. It had been ripped off his wrist when he was flung through the Perspex.

I tracked Basil down – he was then a retired schoolteacher - and spoke to him several times about his great escape. He said that each crew member had been given a synchronised chronometer before the mission and these had to be returned afterwards.

The crash site in 2011

I offered to return this watch to him, but he told me to keep it. It is now on display, with other parts from the crash, at the RAF Memorial Museum at Davidstow.

DATE:	21 DECEMBER 1943
LOCATION/AREA:	NEAR TAVISTOCK
AIRCRAFT TYPE:	HAWKER TYPHOON IB
SERIAL NO:	JR221
SQD/UNIT:	266 SQD / CODE ZH / 12 GROUP
BASE:	DUXFORD
TIME OF CRASH:	16.30HRS
CREW:	F/SGT R. McELROY
PURPOSE OF FLIGHT:	FORMATION CINE GUN PRACTICE
CAUSE OF CRASH:	ENGINE FAILURE

NOTES:

After flying for 1hr 40min, the Typhoon's engine failed and F/Sgt McElroy had to belly land in a field near Tavistock.

When the aircraft was examined, it was found that the auxiliary fuel cock had been turned the wrong way, the pilot thinking it was off. As the auxiliary tank was nearly empty, an airlock had formed causing the engine to fail. This was not the first time this had happened or the last.

F/Sgt McElroy was killed on 19 July 1944.

DATE:	27 DECEMBER 1943
LOCATION/AREA:	HAMEL DOWN
AIRCRAFT TYPE:	CONSOLIDATED B24D
SERIAL NO:	42-40474
SQD/UNIT:	482 BOMB GROUP / EIGHTH AIR FORCE
BASE:	STATION 102 ALCONBURY
TIME OF CRASH:	10.45HRS
CREW:	CAPT R.L.WILLIAMS 1 LT M.L.REMLING 2 LT J.W.HANLEY 2 LT L.F.PETERSON T/SGT J.A.WALLACE T/SGT G.D.WICHNER S/SGT H.D.MACMILLAN S/SGT E.P.RUSH
PURPOSE OF FLIGHT:	TRAINING FLIGHT
CAUSE OF CRASH:	BAD WEATHER AND NAVIGATION ERROR

NOTES: This navigation exercise was training for Operation Carpetbagger, but the B24 was approximately 20 miles south of where it should have been and hit the side of Hamel Down in bad weather killing all on board. There is nothing to see at the site today.

Six of the crew killed while training for Operation Carpetbagger are in this picture – standing, from the left: Milton Remling, Robert Williams, Joseph Hanley (all three died in the crash), Charles Teer. Front, from the left: Eddie Rush, Glenn Wichner (both died in crash), James Beggs, Jesse Wallace (died in crash), Vincent Stuart, T Callahan. (US Airforce)

HAMEL DOWN CARPETBAGGER

A training flight for Operation Carpetbagger ended in disaster when a US Army bomber smashed into the side of Hamel Down killing all eight crew members. It was the third crash on Dartmoor in December 1943 by American aircraft and brought the total number of lives lost to 23.

Operation Carpetbagger was the codename for missions over Europe to drop agents and supplies to help fight the clandestine war against the occupying forces.

The British Special Operations Executive (SOE), set up in July 1940, had been carrying the fight to the enemy through specially trained agents for some time, but now the Americans were in the war, their Office of Strategic Services (OSS)

S/Sgt Henry MacMillan joined the mission at the last minute and lost his life.
(Jerry Simmons)

wanted to be part of the secret war and formed a partnership with the Army Air Forces, SOE and the RAF.

Consolidated Liberator B-24Ds were specially adapted for the missions, but the crews first had to be trained in expert navigation and low flying over land. Therefore each American pilot had to fly two Carpetbagger missions as co-pilot with the RAF on night flights.

Liberator 42-40474 had not yet flown on any Carpetbagger missions, but it is likely that the pilot, Captain Robert Williams, operations officer for the 36th Bomb Squadron, and the three other officers on board had probably flown one or two SOE missions with the RAF as part of their own training.

Williams took off from his Cambridgeshire base at Alconbury at 08.44hrs on 27 December 1943 for a Sunday morning exercise which would take the Liberator to Oxford, Taunton, to Bude Bay on the north Cornwall coast, to 10 miles out from Hartland Point off the north Devon coast and then back to Alconbury.

Last moments of the Carpetbagger training flight. (Author's interpretation)

His crew was made up of 2 Lt Joseph W Hanley, the co-pilot; 1 Lt Milton L Remling, navigator; 2 Lt Louis F Peterson, bombardier; T/Sgt Jesse A. Wallace, engineer; T/Sgt Glen O Wichner, radio operator; S/Sgt Henry D MacMillan, waist gunner, and S/Sgt Eddie P Rush, the tail gunner. MacMillan was not scheduled to be on the training flight, but was pencilled in at the last minute.

The flight went as planned to Taunton, but for some reason the Liberator then veered approximately 20 miles south of the proposed course and headed over Dartmoor where visibility was poor.

Williams was flying a level course at this time and probably believed that he was over Bude Bay, but when he descended through the cloud the giant aircraft crashed onto Hamel Down and burnt.

Local farmers heard the aircraft flying low, but could not see it because of the low cloud.

The salvage team recovered all the bodies. Williams, Hanley, MacMillan, Peterson, Remling and Wichner are buried at the American Cemetery in Cambridge.

What was left of the B24 was taken down the hillside and picked up by trucks.

The official US Army Air Forces accident report gives the time of the crash as 10.45hrs. It says visibility at Exeter and in the vicinity at 10.00hrs was 500yd to 3,000yd. At 11.00hrs at 400ft there was complete cloud cover of the ground, but visibility was given as two miles. However, the words "valley fog" are underlined.

The report says it was not known if the pilot was flying on instruments at the time of the crash.

The report concluded: "The direct cause of the accident is undetermined due to there being no witnesses to the crash, nor was there any part of the wreckage available to the accident committee that they could use to determine the cause.

"It is believed that the pilot possibly was attempting to let down in the bad weather. He was approximately 20 miles south of his proposed course when the ship crashed into one of the hills among the moors.

"There was no means available to the accident committee to determine whether mechanical failure was experienced or not."

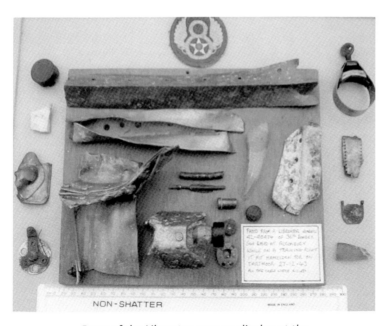

Parts of the Liberator now on display at the
RAF Memorial Museum at Davidstow, Cornwall.

DATE:	28 DECEMBER 1943
LOCATION/AREA:	WOODCOCK HILL
AIRCRAFT TYPE:	CONSOLIDATED PB4Y-1
SERIAL NO:	63926
SQD/UNIT:	VB110 USN
BASE:	DUNKESWELL
TIME OF CRASH:	22.35HRS
CREW:	LT WILLIAM PARISH ENS DONALD LYONS ENS ROGER LOVELACE AMM2 ARTHUR STORK AMM2 JOHN SHAFFER AMM2 LEO DAVENPORT ARM3 JOHN BENSON AOM3 ALFRED RODDY AMM3 CHARLES REYNARD AMM3 DWIGHT NASH
PURPOSE OF FLIGHT:	SEARCH FOR GERMAN DESTROYERS IN BAY OF BISCAY
CAUSE OF CRASH:	BAD WEATHER

NOTES:

The aircraft had been in the air for almost 10 hours when it struck Woodcock Hill and dug a furrow for about a quarter of a mile before falling 400ft into the West Okement Valley and exploding. All the crew were killed. Wreckage was scattered on the hillside, including depth charges, and in the valley below. Some wreckage still remains. There is a small memorial plaque there near one of the engines.

It turned out to be the longest air to submarine attack of the entire war and ended with the courageous captain of a German U-boat scuttling his vessel on a reef off the Spanish coast.

Over a period of nine hours on 10 November 1943, U-966 fought a battle with seven different aircraft until its 24 year-old captain, Ekkehard Wolf, was forced to abandon the submarine, which blew up as its crew were swimming ashore.

Damaged on its maiden voyage, U-966 had no kills and was on its way back to Brest when it was caught on the surface and attacked by a relay of aircraft.

One of these was a PB4Y-1 Liberator 63926 flown by Lt William Parish and one of the depth charges he dropped slowed the submarine down.

Dwight Everett Nash (right) with his twin brother, Clyde, in December 1943. Dwight was killed a few days after this photograph was taken. (Bernard Stevens)

Back at his US Navy VB110 Squadron base at Dunkeswell, near Honiton, Lt Parish posed for a picture with his head poking through the jagged hole in his cockpit caused by a near miss from the U-boat's return fire.

His commanding officer praised Lt Parish and his crew for carrying out the attack in the face of severe anti-aircraft fire and recommended them for awards. But just over six weeks later Lt Parish and his men were all dead – and the awards had to be given posthumously.

For gunner AMM3 Dwight Everett Nash, who had a twin brother in the US Army, there was an Air Medal. His citation reads: "For meritorious achievement while participating in aerial flight as member of the crew aboard a United States Navy bomber attached to Bombing Squadron 110 in action against an enemy submarine in the Bay of Biscay on November 10, 1943. Steadfastly manning his station when his plane sighted the surfaced hostile craft, Nash rendered valuable assistance to his pilot during the subsequent determined and effective attack upon the enemy undersea vessel. His outstanding skill and courageous devotion to duty were in keeping with the highest traditions of the United

The crew of PB4Y-1 Liberator 63926 who lost their lives when the aircraft struck Woodcock Hill and plunged into the West Okement valley – back row, from the left: Bradford, Benson, Davenport, Reynard, Spillman, Shaffer. Front row: Roddy, Lyons, Parish, Lovelace, Nash. Not on the ill-fated patrol were Bradfield and Spillman. (US Navy)

States Naval Service."

It was not submarines but enemy destroyers that Nash and the other crew members of Lt Parish's Liberator had been searching for in the Bay of Biscay on Tuesday 28 December 1943. On their return to base the bomber struck Woodcock Hill in bad weather and dug a furrow for about quarter of a mile before careering 400ft over the edge into the West Okement valley below and blowing up.

The aircraft had been in the air for nine hours and 45 minutes when it hit the high ground at about 22.35hrs. All the crew were killed instantly. Wreckage

Lt William Parish's PB4Y flying very low over the moor. (Author's interpretation)

was left on the hillside above, including some depth charges, but most was in the valley.

Killed with Lt Parish and AMM3C Nash were the co-pilot Ens Donald Lyons; navigator Ens Roger Lovelace, flight engineer AMM2C Arthur Stork; second mechanic AMM2C John Shaffer; first radio operator ARM2C Leo Davenport; second radio operator ARM3C John Benson; ordnance man AOM3C Alfred Roddy and gunner AMM3C Charles Reynard.

There used to be much more wreckage of the Liberator in the West Okement valley as this picture, taken in 1996, shows. The large piece, being held by Peter Foote, is part of the tail fin.

This was the fourth American aircraft to crash on Dartmoor during December 1943. There is an engine and some debris still to be seen there and a small stainless steel plaque has been erected on which the name of Roddy is spelt incorrectly.

After the crash, the Army buried much of the wreckage and tidied up the area, but the many pits to be seen there now are evidence of later searches by souvenir hunters. One of the four Pratt and Whitney engines was recovered by a Torquay based group of enthusiasts in the 1970s.

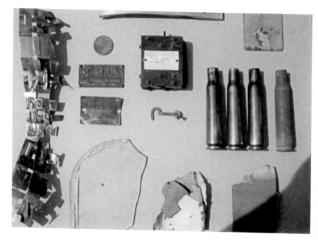

A few parts from the PB4Y-1 on display at the RAF Memorial Museum, Davidstow.

DATE:	5 JANUARY 1944
LOCATION/AREA:	NEAR POSTBRIDGE
AIRCRAFT TYPE:	DE HAVILLAND TIGER MOTH DH82A
SERIAL NO:	DE264
SQD/UNIT:	19 GROUP / CODE G2
BASE:	ROBOROUGH
TIME OF CRASH:	11.45HRS
CREW:	SGT H. N. TROWBRIDGE F/SGT J.P. WORTHINGTON
PURPOSE OF FLIGHT:	TRAINING FLIGHT
CAUSE OF CRASH:	PILOT ERROR

NOTES:

Sgt Trowbridge, the pilot, started a spin during some aerobatics, but below permitted height over high ground. The aircraft crashed and F/Sgt Worthington was killed and the pilot badly injured.

Tiger in trouble above Postbridge. (Author's interpretation)

TIGER DOWN AT POSTBRIDGE

A young pilot's decision to perform aerobatics during a flight over Dartmoor in his squadron's Tiger Moth resulted in a crash which killed his older passenger.

Australians Sgt Harry Trowbridge, 23, and F/Sgt Julian Worthington, 32, were attached to No. 10 Squadron, RAAF, based at RAF Mount Batten, Plymouth. The submarine hunting squadron was part of RAF Coastal Command throughout the war.

It is not clear why the pair were out this particular Wednesday in the Tiger Moth. It may have been a training flight or simply a day off from the stress of war.

The weather on 5 January 1944 was good when Trowbridge and Worthington took off from Roborough for a flight along the Devon coast. Trowbridge had 89 flying hours in his log book, 28 of them on Tiger Moths, and the aircraft he was flying was only two years old.

Trowbridge decided at some stage to indulge in some aerobatics, but he could not pull out of a spin and the biplane crashed at Postbridge, not far from the picturesque waterfall on the East Dart.

Worthington suffered multiple injuries and extensive burns and was killed outright. Trowbridge had a lucky escape, but his left leg was broken in two places, he had a fractured right wrist and also suffered burns and cuts. He was treated at the military hospital at Moretonhampstead.

The cause of the accident was given as the pilot going into a spin below the permitted height over high ground.

Worthington, who came from Mount Albert, Victoria, was buried at Bath. Trowbridge was a warrant officer when he was discharged from service on 3 June 1945. He returned to Australia where he died in 1995.

Parts of the aircraft could be seen at the crash site for some time, but have since been removed.

The famous clapper bridge at Postbridge

DATE:	21 FEBRUARY 1944
LOCATION/AREA:	NEAR HARROWBEER
AIRCRAFT TYPE:	HAWKER TYPHOON 1B
SERIAL NO:	JP962
SQD/UNIT:	266 SQD / CODE ZH
BASE:	HARROWBEER
TIME OF CRASH:	11.20HRS
CREW:	F/SGT H.W.PAUL
PURPOSE OF FLIGHT:	CINE GUN EXERCISE
CAUSE OF CRASH:	ENGINE FAILED

NOTES:

The engine failed after an hour and the pilot force landed near Harrowbeer, writing off the Typhoon. F/Sgt Paul was only slightly injured.

The cause was put down to an airlock caused by both main and auxiliary tanks being switched on at the same time.

DATE:	1 MARCH 1944
LOCATION/AREA:	THREE BARROWS, SOUTH BRENT
AIRCRAFT TYPE:	VICKERS WELLINGTON MKX
SERIAL NO:	LN175
SQD/UNIT:	3 OADU / CODE UNKNOWN
BASE:	HURN, HAMPSHIRE
TIME OF CRASH:	02.00HRS
CREW:	P/O FREDERICK COOKE F/SGT WILLIAM JACK F/SGT ALFRED BEESTON SGT JOHN YEATES
PURPOSE OF FLIGHT:	FERRYING OVERSEAS
CAUSE OF CRASH:	WEATHER/NAVIGATION ERROR

NOTES:

The wrong course was set after take off and the aircraft was 25 miles north of its intended route when it struck a 1,522ft high hill. The wreckage and bodies were found three days later by Sea Cadets out on a ramble.

Small pieces from the crash site, now on display

The crash site of the Wellington near Three Barrows shown to me by Adrian Bunclark, here on his mobility scooter

DATE:	17 APRIL 1944
LOCATION/AREA:	HARROWBEER
AIRCRAFT TYPE:	HAWKER HURRICANE MKI
SERIAL NO:	L1715
SQD/UNIT:	691 SQD / CODE 55
BASE:	ROBOROUGH
TIME OF CRASH:	19.15HRS
CREW:	P/O J. KOZICKI (POL)
PURPOSE OF FLIGHT:	NAVY CO-OPERATION EXERCISE
CAUSE OF CRASH:	ENGINE FAULT

NOTES:

As P/O Kozicki came in to land at Roborough, he found the throttle would not close. He made several attempts to land, but then decided to fly to Harrowbeer which had longer runways. He flew along the longest runway and as he reached the last quarter, the engine cut and he made a forced landing. He was slightly injured.

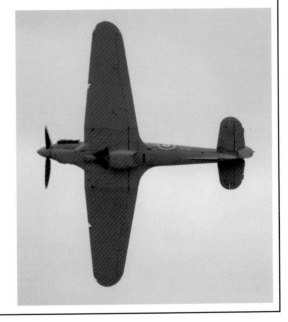

Mk I Hawker Hurricane

DATE:	28 MAY 1944
LOCATION/AREA:	YELVERTON
AIRCRAFT TYPE:	HAWKER TYPHOON 1B
SERIAL NO:	EK211
SQD/UNIT:	263 SQD / CODE HE
BASE:	HARROWBEER
TIME OF CRASH:	DAYTIME
CREW:	F/SGT JACK PRINGLE
PURPOSE OF FLIGHT:	BOMBING EXERCISE
CAUSE OF CRASH:	UNKNOWN

NOTES:

F/Sgt Pringle, 21, took off from Harrowbeer but did not gain height quickly enough and clipped the top of the 65ft tower of Yelverton (St Paul's) Church. The aircraft went out of control and crashed into a field nearby, killing the pilot. His body was returned to County Antrim, Northern Ireland, for burial.

Pilot's tribute: a plaque at Yelverton Church

DATE:	29 MAY 1944
LOCATION/AREA:	TROWLESWORTHY TOR
AIRCRAFT TYPE:	BRISTOL BEAUFIGHTER MK VI
SERIAL NO:	MM843
SQD/UNIT:	406 SQD / CODE HU / 10 GROUP
BASE:	WINKLEIGH
TIME OF CRASH:	00.20HRS
CREW:	P/O P.W. MAAS (RCAF) F/O A. DUNCAN (RCAF)
PURPOSE OF FLIGHT:	SEARCHLIGHT CO-OPERATION
CAUSE OF CRASH:	ELEVATOR FAULT

NOTES:

While flying over Plymouth, the pilot experienced elevator trouble and told his navigator to bale out while he tried unsuccessfully to regain control before baling out himself. Both men were unhurt.

Looking towards Trowlesworthy Tor.

LOST CONTROL

A Monday night searchlight co-operation exercise over Plymouth almost ended in disaster for two young Canadians – all because of faulty rivets.

Their Beaufighter blew itself apart when crashing near Trowlesworthy Tor after the two-man crew had to bale out when the pilot found he could not control the aircraft.

Winkleigh airfield in West Devon was the base in May 1944 for the Canadians of 406 Night Fighter Squadron equipped with the Mk VI F Bristol Beaufighter.

Their motto was "We Kill By Night" and one crew had recently shot down three Dornier 217s over Devon in one night. This was mainly due to the top secret intercept radar fitted in a thimble-like structure on the nose of the Beaufighter.

On 29 May 1944, two of the squadron's Beaufighters were to take part in a searchlight exercise over Plymouth during which the operators of the searchlights would try to cone the night fighters in their beams.

At the controls of Beaufighter MM843 was P/O P. W. Maas, with F/O A. Duncan as his navigator. They took off at 23.30hrs and then spent 50 minutes twisting and turning over Plymouth trying to evade the searchlight beams.

Another Bristol Beaufighter showing the thimble nose radome protecting the centimetric radar. (Bristol)

A searchlight exercise for Bristol Beaufighter
MM843 goes wrong. (Author's interpretation)

It was 20 minutes after midnight when P/O Maas suddenly found the elevators of the aircraft would not work and at 13,000ft he ordered his navigator to bale out. The pilot tried three times to regain control of the Beaufighter without success before he too baled out at 9,000ft.

The Beaufighter lit up the sky when it exploded on impact while the two Canadians came down safely near Lee Moor where they were looked after by local farmers.

The RAF sent transport from Harrowbeer to pick them up and they spent the rest of the night at the airfield before being returned to Winkleigh the following day.

Air crash investigators from Farnborough came down to check over the wreckage and on the elevators they found that the rivets holding the rib flanges to the torque tube had sheared off causing the elevators to become inoperable. These rivets were made of aluminium and after this accident a modification was issued.

Nothing remains at the site today. A man who lived at Roborough told me he had picked up a few parts of the Beaufighter in the 1950s, but I have not seen them.

DATE:	11 JULY 1944
LOCATION/AREA:	HARROWBEER
AIRCRAFT TYPE:	SUPERMARINE SPITFIRE MKIX LF
SERIAL NO:	MJ291
SQD/UNIT:	64 SQD /CODE SH / 11 GROUP
BASE:	HARROWBEER
TIME OF CRASH:	11.15HRS
CREW:	F/SGT W.A.LIVESEY
PURPOSE OF FLIGHT:	RECONNAISSANCE
CAUSE OF CRASH:	ENGINE FAILURE

NOTES:

Returning from a shipping reconnaissance, the Spitfire's engine cut out at 700ft and F/Sgt Livesey had no choice but to force land 300yds short of the runway with his wheels up. He was only slightly injured. The aircraft was written off but the engine was used for spares.

Ground Staff refuel a Spitfire Mk VB of 64 Squadron in May 1942

DATE:	20 JULY 1944
LOCATION/AREA:	HARROWBEER
AIRCRAFT TYPE:	SUPERMARINE SPITFIRE MKIXB
SERIAL NO:	NH340
SQD/UNIT:	126 SQD / CODE BV / 10 GROUP
BASE:	CULMHEAD
TIME OF CRASH:	07.15HRS
CREW:	F/O J.S. DAVIDSON (RAAF)
PURPOSE OF FLIGHT:	RECONNAISSANCE
CAUSE OF CRASH:	PILOT ERROR

NOTES:

F/O Davidson approached the runway too fast and at an angle on his return from his shipping reconnaissance patrol so made the decision to go around again. He opened the throttle, but his Spitfire was already very low and struck a parked Spitfire NH402 and crashed. Both aircraft were written off, but the pilot escaped with only slight injuries.

A Spitfire MK 1X

DATE:	12 SEPTEMBER 1944
LOCATION/AREA:	LEE MOOR
AIRCRAFT TYPE:	SHORT STIRLING MKIII
SERIAL NO:	LK499
SQD/UNIT:	1653 HCU / CODE H4 / 3 GROUP
BASE:	CHEDBURGH, SUFFOLK
TIME OF CRASH:	22.45HRS
CREW:	F/O NORMAN McDONALD (RCAF) F/O SAMUEL McGUIGAN (RCAF) F/O ROGER MURPHY SGT LAWRENCE BOWD SGT GEORGE CANHAM SGT GEORGE BENNETT SGT THOMAS HUNTER
PURPOSE OF FLIGHT:	CROSS-COUNTRY TRAINING
CAUSE OF CRASH:	STRUCTURAL FAILURE

NOTES:

This aircraft had completed 16 operations, two of which were for SOE, before being taken off squadron. All the crew were killed when the tail unit broke off and it dived into soft ground and exploded.

LEE MOOR STIRLING

An uncomfortable pilot's seat harness may have caused a spate of Stirling bomber crashes, including one at Lee Moor in which the seven man crew were all killed.

The tail of Stirling LK499 broke off after it went out of control during a cross country training exercise and the giant bomber buried itself into the ground.

This Stirling Mark III had been built by the Austin Motor Company at Longbridge, sub-contractors for Shorts of Belfast. The Mark III, which boasted a nose turret, weighed well over 30 tons. The 87ft long fuselage was built in three sections and the wingspan measured 99ft. With a bomb load of eight tons, the Stirling could not reach high altitudes which meant it was vulnerable to flak on its raids into Germany.

Stirling LK499 was delivered to 149 Squadron at Mildenhall on 22 February 1944 and after 16 successful missions over Europe, the aircraft passed into the hands of 1653 Heavy Conversion Unit (HCU) at Chedburgh, Suffolk, on 3 May.

A Tuesday night cross country training exercise was planned for 12 September 1944 involving LK499 and two other Stirlings. They took off at 21.15hrs and headed to the north west over Rugby, then south west for Bristol and then a course for Plymouth was flown.

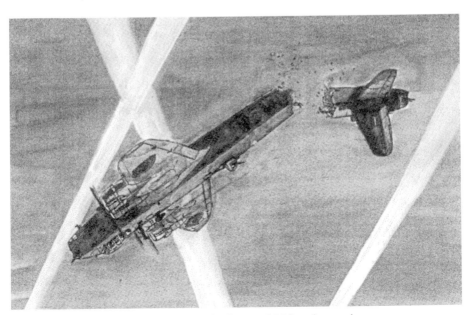

Disaster in the sky for the former SOE bomber and crew when the tail unit broke off. (Author's interpretation)

The crash site at Lee Moor

At the controls of the ill-fated Stirling was pupil pilot F/O Norman MacDonald, aged 25, from Ontario, Canada. He had flown 32 hours on Stirlings, 10 of these at night. Instructing him was F/O Roger Murphy, who had been posted to the HCU after completing his tour of duty. There were some pilots who thought this instructing role was more dangerous than combat missions.

The navigator was another Canadian, F/O Samuel McGuigan, 23, who gave a new course north from Plymouth. All the other crew members were English. They were flight engineer Sgt Thomas Hunter, air gunner Sgt Lawrence Bowd, 20, wireless operator Sgt George Canham, 22, and air gunner Sgt George Bennett, 19.

For some reason, LK 499 went out of control and into a dive which caused the tail unit to break off and the big bomber arrowed into the ground near the clay works at 22.45hrs.

When locals reached the crash site it was obvious nothing could be done to save the crew. A trail of wreckage was blocking the road when police and the Home Guard arrived. The wreck was cordoned off and the Home Guard spent the night there to prevent looting.

The next day the grim search for bodies and clues to what caused the tragedy began. The bulk of the aircraft had buried itself in the clay and the wreckage lay scattered 900 yards to the west with the tail at the end.

Back at Farnborough, the chief inspector of the RAF Accident Investigation Branch, Air Commodore Vernon Brown, was inquiring into other Stirling losses in which the tail units had broken off while in a dive.

He discovered that Stirling pilots did not like the seat harness fitted and after take-off would remove it. However, this could cause the pilot to fall over the control column when the aircraft was put in a dive producing what is known as a bunt, an inverted loop in which massive forces would be put on the airframe and the crew would have difficulty baling out.

The body of the pilot, F/O MacDonald, was found some distance from the wreck and he was buried at Brookwood Cemetery, Surrey, and the bodies of Sgts Bowd, Canham, Hunter and Bennett were taken for burial in their home towns.

Sgt Jones, F/O Murphy and F/O McGuigan were not found at the time and they are listed on the Runnymede Memorial, but a local doctor and a fireman later revealed that some remains were discovered and had been taken to Plymouth and buried in one grave as unknown airmen.

The crash produced a most difficult and dangerous recovery for the Taunton-based 67 Maintenance Unit. They located the starboard inner engine, but it disappeared overnight and was found next day to be 3ft deeper in the clay.

The Air Investigations Branch were satisfied with the parts that had been salvaged and, having dug down to about 14ft when normal salvage became impossible, the MU were able to abandon the three remaining engines and fill in the craters.

Many years ago, a local man took me to the crash site where a few Stirling parts were found beside the road.

Since then the remains of this aircraft have been recovered and a large trench can be seen. It is not known who recovered the rest of the aircraft, but they must have used heavy diggers. At one stage, the clay works wanted to extend into this area, but bowed to public protest and the area is now safe for people to enjoy.

Canadian navigator
F/O Samuel McGuigan

DATE:	8 JUNE 1945
LOCATION/AREA:	SOUTH BRENT
AIRCRAFT TYPE:	AIRSPEED OXFORD MKI
SERIAL NO:	PH145
SQD/UNIT:	691 SQD / CODE SS
BASE:	HARROWBEER
TIME OF CRASH:	UNKNOWN
CREW:	SGT K. T. BAKAS LAC C. P. HEAPS (RAFVR)
PURPOSE OF FLIGHT:	UNKNOWN
CAUSE OF CRASH:	UNAUTHORISED LOW FLYING HIT HIGH TENSION CABLES

NOTES: While returning to Harrowbeer the pilot decided to carry out some low flying and hit high tension cables and crashed, killing both crewmen.

The Polish Air Force pilot, Kazimierz Tadeusz Bakas, aged 30, is buried at Plymouth (Weston Mill) Cemetery. His passenger, LAC Cyril Parkin Heaps, 21, is buried in Anfield Cemetery, Liverpool.

Airspeed Oxford Mk1

DATE:	16 JULY 1945
LOCATION/AREA:	HARROWBEER
AIRCRAFT TYPE:	DE HAVILLAND MOSQUITO NF30
SERIAL NO:	MM734
SQD/UNIT:	406 SQD /CODE HU
BASE:	WINKLEIGH
TIME OF CRASH:	EARLY EVENING
CREW:	F/O ROBERT SLOAN (RCAF) F/SGT GORDON MOIR (RCAF)
PURPOSE OF FLIGHT:	CROSS COUNTRY
CAUSE OF CRASH:	LOW ON FUEL

NOTES:

The war in Europe had been over for just over two months, but training went on for crews. Mosquito MM734, with 406 Squadron newcomers F/O Robert Sloan and F/Sgt Gordon Moir as crew, approached Harrowbeer low on fuel after an afternoon cross-country exercise. However, on landing a wing tip hit a dispersal bay which resulted in the Mosquito crashing and burning out.

A Mosquito NF30 like the one that crashed at Harrowbeer

F/O Robert Sloan

F/Sgt Gordon Moir

The pilot, F/O Sloan, was killed instantly and although F/Sgt Moir was pulled clear, he died 90 minutes later. They had been with their squadron for just over a month.

The next day, S/Ldr Don MacFadyen DSO, DFC & Bar and F/Sgt Underwood came down to investigate the incident. They found that the pilot had committed too violent turns near the ground to line up with the wrong runway.

Two days after the crash, two pilots flew to Blackbushe airfield in Hampshire for the funerals. Moir had served in the Irish Fusiliers and retrained as a pilot.

This Canadian squadron was disbanded at the end of the following month.

DATE:	12 MAY 1945
LOCATION/AREA:	HARROWBEER
AIRCRAFT TYPE:	NORTH AMERICAN MUSTANG MKI
SERIAL NO:	AP219
SQD/UNIT:	26 SQD /CODE XC
BASE:	HARROWBEER
TIME OF CRASH:	08.35 HRS
CREW:	F/LT R.C.H.JONES
PURPOSE OF FLIGHT:	PHOTO RECONNAISSANCE
CAUSE OF CRASH:	PILOT ERROR

NOTES:

F/Lt Jones, with five other aircraft, had taken part in
a photo reconnaissance mission before British troops
regained the Channel Islands.

On landing, he was caught in the slipstream of the
preceding aircraft. He opened up to overshoot, but at the
last minute decided to land. Unable to stop on the wet
grass, he ran into a dispersal bay and hit and killed LAC
A. Mastin, an electrician, who was working there. The pilot
was injured and the Mustang written off.

*The Channel Islands were under German occupation
from 1940 until liberated by British forces in 1945.*

Aerial photography of the Channel Islands

DATE:	13 OCTOBER 1945
LOCATION/AREA:	HUNTINGDON WARREN
AIRCRAFT TYPE:	DOUGLAS C-47 SKYTRAIN
SERIAL NO:	42-100640
SQD/UNIT:	484 AIR SERVICE GROUP
BASE:	EUROPEAN AIR DEPOT ERDING, GERMANY
TIME OF CRASH:	16.10HRS
CREW:	2 LT R.H.MARA 2 LT F.G.McCUTCHIN F/ENG M.J.KACK LT COL C.R.RASMUSSEN PFC R.FLOWER PFC D.L.KLAPPS PVT V.E.WHITING
PURPOSE OF FLIGHT:	PASSENGER AND MAIL DROP AT EXETER
CAUSE OF CRASH:	BAD WEATHER AND CONTROL GAVE INCORRECT HEADING

NOTES: Weather conditions deteriorated and Exeter informed 2 Lt Mara that he would be unable to land there. They gave him an incorrect heading to Westonzoyland, Somerset, and the Skytrain flew in the wrong direction and crashed in mist near the former home of the rabbit warrener. The three crew members and four passengers were all killed.

An example of a C47 in flight

HEADING FOR DISASTER

All pilots of the 484th Air Service Group Command were ordered to double check information received from ground stations following the deaths of seven Americans in an air crash two months after the end of the war.

Their Douglas C-47 Skytrain struck the hillside in thick mist and then ploughed into the wall of a field near the Huntingdon Warren house after the pilot had been given the wrong heading to a diversionary airfield.

The former Luftwaffe pilot training base near Erding, not far from Munich, was home to the 9th Army Air Force, which was part of the 484th Group Command. Its role was to ferry service personnel and equipment back to the UK and then on to the United States.

The Skytrain had taken off just after midday on Saturday 13 October 1945 from Erding, with a crew of three and four passengers - plus mail - bound for RAF Exeter.

The pilot was 29-year-old 2 Lt Richard Mara, with 2 Lt Francis McCutchin as the co-pilot and T/Sgt Melvin Kack as the flight engineer. Both pilots were experienced men.

This is the wall near the Huntingdon Warren house hit by the Skytrain

Their passengers were Lt Col Clifford Rasmussen, of the 4020th AAC Base Unit at Wright Field, Ohio, Pvt Victor Whiting, Pfc Ralph Flower and Pfc Dominick Klapps.

The story of the final hours of flight 42-100640 was revealed at a subsequent inquiry into the crash.

A routine trip turned into tragedy when the weather began closing in over Devon and the flying control officer at Exeter told Lt Mara that Exeter was enveloped in fog and he would not be able to land there.

Lt Mara asked for an alternative landing field and was told he could land at Westonzoyland, four miles from Bridgwater.

The pilot then asked Exeter for the distance to the Somerset airfield, the type of terrain he could expect there and the magnetic heading. This was given to him as 235 degrees – incredibly this was 180 degrees incorrect to Westonzoyland and no one on the Skytrain, which was flying on instruments at the time, queried this.

The aircraft, as a result, flew drastically off course and at 16.10hrs crashed in mist into the hillside near Huntingdon Warren house and partly through the wall of the top field.

Communication with the Skytrain had been good, despite the weather, and when no more was heard from Lt Mara it was assumed the aircraft had crashed.

The cross embedded in a boulder above the warren house

There were no witnesses to the crash, but several heard the sound of an aircraft flying low over the moor and this helped the authorities when they began the search. A police team found the bodies and wreckage the next day.

Pfc Flower is buried at the American military cemetery in Cambridge while all the other bodies were returned to the United States.

While researching the crash I was told an interesting story by a local man. He was a small boy at the time and went to the site soon after the crash with his father who was a fireman. He

Heading for disaster: the final seconds of the Skytrain. (Author's interpretation)

told me that there were bundles of English banknotes among the wreckage. Policemen were gathering it up and he was told not to touch it and that it was all counterfeit.

If you visit the crash site, look for a large boulder above the ruined warren house and you may find one of Dartmoor's smallest crosses embedded firmly in it. It was made at school and fixed there in 1985 by schoolboy Brett Sutherland, with the help of his father, as a tribute to those who lost their lives in the crash.

The ruins of the house at Huntingdon Warren, near the Skytrain crash site.

NOTES:	3 JANUARY 1947
LOCATION/AREA:	PLYMSTOCK
AIRCRAFT TYPE:	SUPERMARINE SPITFIRE XV1
SERIAL NO:	TE253
SQD/UNIT:	691 SQD AAC / CODE 55
BASE:	CHIVENOR/HARROWBEER
TIME OF CRASH:	10.40HRS
CREW:	W/O ANTHONY CHARLES GREEN
PURPOSE OF FLIGHT:	NAVY CO-OPERATION EXERCISE
CAUSE OF CRASH:	BAD WEATHER

NOTES:

This exercise was brought to a premature end by bad weather and W/O Green's Spitfire was seen to fly low over a road before crashing into a field and exploding. The pilot was thrown from the aircraft and killed.

W/O Green, who came from Woodford Green, Essex, was just 22 years old. He is buried at Heaton Punchardon, North Devon.

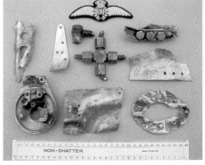

The Spitfire crash site on the edge of the moor   *All that is left now of the Spitfire*

DATE:	18 JUNE 1947
LOCATION/AREA:	CORNWOOD
AIRCRAFT TYPE:	FAIREY FIREFLY FRI
SERIAL NO:	PP533
SQD/UNIT:	746 SQD
BASE:	ST MERRYN, CORNWALL
TIME OF CRASH:	UNKNOWN
CREW:	LT HAROLD DEREK EASY DSC CAPT P.J. WADDINGTON
PURPOSE OF FLIGHT:	UNKNOWN
CAUSE OF CRASH:	BAD WEATHER

NOTES:

Both the Fleet Air Arm pilot and his Army passenger were killed when the Firefly crashed in poor visibility into a wood at Cornwood and burst into flames. Lt Easy was 25 and left a widow. St Merryn was commissioned as HMS Vulture in August 1940 and was the first wartime airfield to open in Cornwall

The headstones of Lt Harold Easy (top left) and Capt. P.J. Waddington (bottom left)

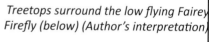

Treetops surround the low flying Fairey Firefly (below) (Author's interpretation)

DATE:	23 OCTOBER 1947
LOCATION/AREA:	BRENT MOOR
AIRCRAFT TYPE:	SUPERMARINE SPITFIRE XVI
SERIAL NO:	TE406
SQD/UNIT:	203 AFS/ CODE JH
BASE:	CHIVENOR
TIME OF CRASH:	MORNING
CREW:	P/O A.R.GRAHAM
PURPOSE OF FLIGHT:	RECCE TRAINING FLIGHT
CAUSE OF CRASH:	BAD WEATHER

NOTES:

While flying on instruments, P/O Alexander Graham turned to starboard to fly on a reciprocal course, but lost height in the turn. The wing hit the ground and the aircraft cartwheeled and broke up.

The grave of P/O Alexander Graham in Crosthwaite churchyard, Keswick.

HEARTBREAK ON BRENT MOOR

To lose a young son to war is one thing, but to lose one after the war is over must have been doubly hard for Mungo and Jane Graham, of Portinscale, near Derwent Water in Cumbria.

Their 21 year-old pilot officer son was found dead in the burnt out remains of his Mark XVI Spitfire on Brent Moor after failing to return from a reconnaissance training flight over Devon.

P/O Alexander Robert Graham was from the 203 Advanced Flying School based at RAF Chivenor. At 1600hrs on Thursday 23 October 1947, he took off from the North Devon airfield in Spitfire TE406. He should have returned at about 17.15hrs, but when he did not appear a search began involving air-sea rescue launches, aircraft and the police.

The next day, another pilot from Chivenor, F/Lt G. Barber, spotted the burnt out wreckage on Brent Moor while carrying out an air search.

Rescuers guided to the spot found the remains of the Spitfire with the young pilot still in the cockpit. His body was taken by RAF ambulance to the mortuary at Totnes where he was formally identified by his commanding officer.

An inquest at Totnes, held three days later, heard F/Lt Barber say that he spotted the burnt out Spitfire at about 12.40hrs the day after it had gone missing. He told the coroner that P/O Graham was "a very qualified pilot" and that this was his third flight in a Spitfire.

The cause of the accident is not certain, but while flying on instruments in poor weather, P/O Graham may have lost height in a turn to starboard with the wing hitting the ground and the aircraft cartwheeling.

He is buried in Crosthwaite churchyard, Keswick.

DATE:	23 JULY 1948
LOCATION/AREA:	DEAN PRIOR
AIRCRAFT TYPE:	SUPERMARINE SPITFIRE XVI
SERIAL NO:	SL618
SQD/UNIT:	203 AFS / CODE HX
BASE:	CHIVENOR
TIME OF CRASH:	13.55HRS
CREW:	PIV R.F. ATKINSON
PURPOSE OF FLIGHT:	DUTY SECTOR RECCE
CAUSE OF CRASH:	ENGINE FAILURE

NOTES:

This pilot suffered an engine failure after the con rod broke and he selected a field in which to make a forced landing. He was skidding too fast after he landed and tried to avoid a hedge at the end of the field by putting the starboard wing down, but the aircraft struck the hedge, ripping the starboard wing off, and the Spitfire came to rest 100 yards further on. The pilot escaped injury.

PIV stood for pilot class four, part of the RAF ranks experimented with from 1947.

DATE:	12 MARCH 1953
LOCATION/AREA:	PLYMPTON RD, IVYBRIDGE
AIRCRAFT TYPE:	SUPERMARINE SPITFIRE MK XXI
SERIAL NO:	LA190
SQD/UNIT:	3 CAACU / 62 SOUTHERN GROUP
BASE:	EXETER
TIME OF CRASH:	11.10HRS
CREW:	MR ALEC INCE
PURPOSE OF FLIGHT:	ROUTINE FLIGHT
CAUSE OF CRASH:	ENGINE FAILURE

NOTES:

The engine began to run rough at less than 2,000ft. The pilot, an instructor flying alone, could not maintain height at full throttle so made a wheels-up landing in a field.

Alec Ince pancaked into a field

TWO DOWN IN FIVE MINUTES

Two former RAF pilots had to force land their aircraft within five minutes of each other after both had taken off from Exeter for the same Thursday exercise.

Both aircraft also came from 3 Civilian Anti-Aircraft Co-operation Unit (CAACU).

The first aircraft was a Mk XX1 Spitfire, serial number LA190, which was one of 21 built. It was delivered to Farnborough on 18 August 1944 for research and development. From here it went to Boscombe Down - here a Griffon 61 engine was fitted – and used for landing trials. After this it was sent back to Vickers before going to 3 CAACU on 8 October 1951.

Former flight lieutenant Alec A. Ince, a civilian instructor with the RAF, was at the controls of the Spitfire for an exercise with the Royal Navy on 12 March 1953. He had 1,819 hours in his log book, 450 of them on Spitfires.

He took off at 10.42hrs, but after 20 minutes at 2,000ft the engine started to run rough and the loss of power was so bad that the aircraft began to lose height.

The pilot told Exeter of his problem and then picked a field near Lee Mill for a wheels-up landing, which he achieved successfully without any injury. Two farm workers, a Mr Hill and a Mr Maddock, watched the Spitfire force land and they ran to the aid of Mr Ince. They took him to the farmhouse from where he called Exeter and the police.

The Spitfire was broken up and sold for scrap five days later.

A Spitfire XXI like the one that force landed at Ivybridge

A Bristol Beaufighter Mark X (Bristol)

The other aircraft forced down was a twin-engine Bristol Beaufighter Mk X, serial number RD 849, which was involved in the same exercise. It was being flown by former RAF sergeant G. M. File, also of 3 CAACU, who had 2,053 hours in his log book, 220 on Beaufighters.

He had taken off before the Spitfire, at 09.45hrs, but an hour and 25 minutes into the exercise the port air screw failed to feather when tested in flight. Then the engine began to over speed, which caused a lot of drag.

Mr File could not fly the Beaufighter without dropping the nose. He was losing height and realised he would not make it back to Exeter so he selected a stubble field near Dean Prior and, with the port air screw wind milling, he made a forced landing.

He had come down at 11.15hrs – just five minutes after the Spitfire. Mr File was uninjured and he too was helped by farm workers who took him to a farm from where he contacted Exeter airfield, police and fire brigade.

The Beaufighter was cordoned off in case of fire and later broken up for scrap. Nowadays we would consider scrapping a Spitfire and Beaufighter as sacrilege, but in the 1950s a glut of wartime aircraft meant it was not worth repairing aircraft that had force landed.

There is nothing to be found at the sites today.

DATE:	12 MARCH 1953
LOCATION/AREA:	DEAN PRIOR
AIRCRAFT TYPE:	BRISTOL BEAUFIGHTER MK10
SERIAL NO:	RD849
SQD/UNIT:	3 CAACU
BASE:	EXETER
TIME OF CRASH:	11.15HRS
CREW:	MR G.M.FILE
PURPOSE OF FLIGHT:	NAVY CO-OPERATION EXERCISE
CAUSE OF CRASH:	FAULTY PORT ENGINE

NOTES:

The civilian pilot had to make a forced landing in a field after the port air screw failed to feather when tested in flight and began to over speed. The ex RAF man escaped injury.

A 1950s line-up of 3 CAACU at Exeter. Mr Reg Graham, who gave me the photograph, is fourth from the left in the back row

DATE:	29 FEBRUARY 1956
LOCATION/AREA:	CADOVER BRIDGE
AIRCRAFT TYPE:	BOULTON PAUL BALLIOL T2
SERIAL NO:	WN517
SQD/UNIT:	238 OCU
BASE:	COLERNE
TIME OF CRASH:	10.10HRS
CREW:	F/SGT DONALD TOOGOOD
PURPOSE OF FLIGHT:	INTERCEPTION EXERCISE
CAUSE OF CRASH:	ENGINE FAILURE

NOTES:

A crankshaft fracture is thought to have caused this fatal crash which followed several Mayday distress calls by F/Sgt Toogood, who was involved in an exercise with another Balliol WN517. F/Sgt Toogood had informed this attacking aircraft that his engine was running rough and he would return to base.

F/Sgt Toogood had qualified in 1946 to fly Lancasters.

Boulton Paul Balliol showing folding wings for reduced storage

"MAYDAY, MAYDAY"

The tragic final moments in the life of F/Sgt Donald George Toogood were recalled at an inquest following his death in an aircraft crash near Cadover Bridge on 29 February 1956.

The 30-year-old experienced flier and father of two issued several Mayday distress calls before his radio went silent.

F/Sgt Toogood was a member of 238 Operational Conversion Unit based at RAF Colerne in Wiltshire, where pilots and navigators were trained to work together as crews of night fighters. He had logged 4,700 hours of flying and was highly thought of.

He took off in a Boulton Paul Balliol T2 WN517 early on this Wednesday morning to act as a target aircraft in an interception exercise. He had been in the air for two hours when he informed the attacking aircraft that his engine was sounding rough and he would return to base.

The dramatic story of what happened next was reported by the Tavistock Times at the inquest into F/Sgt Toogood's death.

Lt/Cdr W. Hawley, of RNAS Culdrose, was flying south of the Lizard at the time when he heard a Mayday distress call from another aircraft.

"The flier gave his position as near Exmouth at about 9,000ft up. He said his

Firemen hose down the smouldering wreckage of the Balliol (anon)

engine was cutting out. He thought the trouble was in his constant speed unit," recalled Lt/Cdr Hawley.

"Someone answered him, I don't know who. It may have been Gloucester, but someone answered his Mayday call and gave him a course to steer by. Shortly afterwards I heard him say that he could not maintain his altitude. He continued to descend.

"He acknowledged calls from an unknown ground station until he reached 5,000ft. At this altitude he gave another Mayday call and stated that his engine had failed completely. Then he followed this by saying he was going into cloud and descending rapidly. He gave a further Mayday call and then silence."

F/Lt K. G. Richards told the inquest that F/Sgt Toogood was in his flight and was an above average pilot. He said a court of inquiry would investigate the crash and why the engine failed. The aircraft had been used during the week and was in a good condition.

When asked by the coroner why the F/Sgt had not baled out, F/Lt Richards said this decision was always left to the pilot, but he pointed out that F/Sgt Toogood did not know where he was.

Maj Hugh McLean, of the 1st Battalion Somerset Light Infantry, Seaton Barracks, Plymouth, told the coroner that he was on an exercise when he heard the backfiring of an approaching aircraft. It had appeared suddenly out of the mist with a trail of smoke coming from the engine. It lost height rapidly, skimming over some trees and crashing in a large burst of flame.

He and another officer drove to the wreckage but were unable to approach nearer than five yards owing to the flames. He could see the figure of a man in the cockpit. He was sitting still with his head thrown back and was unconscious. He was of the opinion that his neck was broken. Flames were coming from both wings.

"There was nothing we could do to help," said the Major.

The coroner returned a verdict of accidental death. He said that the pilot died from a fractured skull and the burns were received after he had died.

F/Sgt Toogood is buried in Colerne churchyard. There is nothing to see at the crash site today.

DATE:	31 MAY 1965
LOCATION/AREA:	FLAT TOR PAN
AIRCRAFT TYPE:	DE HAVILLAND SEA VIXEN FAW 1
SERIAL NO:	XN648
SQD/UNIT:	766 SQD / CODE VL716
BASE:	RNAS YEOVILTON
TIME OF CRASH:	15.25HRS
CREW	SUB LT DEREK COTTRILL SUB LT ROY KENWARD
PURPOSE OF FLIGHT:	COMBAT EXERCISE
CAUSE OF CRASH:	ENGINE FAULT

NOTES: The Sea Vixen was taking part in a combat exercise with two other Sea Vixens from the Somerset base when the pilot, Sub Lt Cottrill, reported a serious fault with the engine. He contacted the other two aircraft and contact was also made with RAF Chivenor who sent a rescue helicopter to the area.

Pilot and observer ejected over Cut Hill and were soon picked up by the helicopter while their aircraft flew on before diving into the boggy ground at Flat Tor Pan, near the East Dart.

A salvage team turned up the next day to find a large crater and they did what they could to clear wreckage, but most of the aircraft is still buried in the ground below what is now a large pond.

Further clean ups have been done over the years as bits and pieces have come to the surface.

Sea Vixen XN648 at RNAS Yeovilton (Royal Navy)

This pond marks the crash site of the Sea Vixen at Flat Tor Pan

A photograph taken from the RAF Chivenor rescue helicopter of the two crewmen waiting to be picked up. The crewman on the right still has his helmet on. (RAF Chivenor)

DATE:	24 MARCH 1966
LOCATION/AREA:	GREAT FRENCHBEER, CHAGFORD
AIRCRAFT TYPE:	DE HAVILLAND SEA VIXEN FAW 1
SERIAL NO:	XJ522
SQD/UNIT:	766 SQD / TAIL CODE VL
BASE:	RNAS YEOVILTON
TIME OF CRASH:	15.25HRS
CREW:	SUB LT I. McKECHNIE SUB LT E. HUGHES
PURPOSE OF FLIGHT:	FIGHTER TACTICS EXERCISE
CAUSE OF CRASH:	MID AIR COLLISION

NOTES:

A training exercise over Fernworthy Reservoir went wrong when Sea Vixen XJ522 lost its nose after a collision with the tail of Sea Vixen XJ513 and the crew had to eject. The other Sea Vixen returned to base without realising the tail was damaged.

Sea Vixen XJ522 on board the Ark Royal. (Royal Navy)

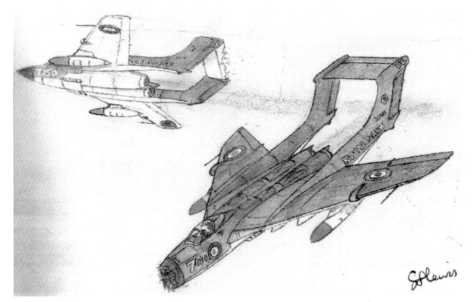

Aftermath of the collision (Author's interpretation)

CHAGFORD MID-AIR COLLISION

A mid-air collision between two jets over a Dartmoor reservoir resulted in the crew of one jet ejecting safely and the other jet landing back at base - with its crew blissfully unaware that it was missing part of the tail!

Four Sea Vixens from the Naval Air Fighter School (766 Squadron) at RNAS Yeovilton were to take part in a fighter tactics and combat air patrol sortie on Thursday 24 March 1966 over Fernworthy reservoir. The Sea Vixens were to attack the dam while four Hawker Hunters from RAF Chivenor tried to stop them.

When the Hunters attacked, Sea Vixens returning from other sorties joined the melee and upwards of 12 aircraft were engaged in a dogfight over the reservoir - what a sight that must have been.

A similar exercise had been flown at low level by other aircraft earlier in the day, but as the weather had deteriorated slightly, this exercise was to be carried out at medium level.

Sub Lt Ian McKechnie and his navigator, Sub Lt Ed Hughes, were in Sea Vixen XJ522 while Sub Lt Chas Hussey and Ralph Magnus, a US Navy officer on exchange, were in Sea Vixen XJ513.

The much decorated Capt Ian McKechnie

During the dogfight, Yeovilton heard over the radio two pilots claiming a "kill" on a Hunter. This turned out to be McKechnie and Hussey who, at 16.20hrs, had gone for the same "enemy" aircraft and were now in the same piece of sky.

The nose of Sub Lt McKechnie's XJ522 caught the tail of Sub Lt Hussey's XJ513 hard. The nose broke off and the two crewmen quickly ejected at 25,000ft.

Hughes came down in gorse which dragged his parachute to a stop, but McKechnie's parachute had collapsed in a down- draught and he hit the ground hard, damaging his back and one of his knees.

Forestry workers witnessed the incident and picked up both men with a tractor and trailer and took them to nearby Collihole Farm, where they were given cups of tea. Meanwhile, their aircraft crashed near Great Frenchbeer.

Sub Lt Hussey was not aware of the damage to his aircraft and when he landed at Yeovilton and was taxiing past the control tower they asked him if he knew his tail was badly damaged.

RAF Chivenor sent a helicopter, with a doctor on board, to collect McKechnie and Edwards, but with the wind picking up and five on board, the pilot said he would not be able to make it back to Yeovilton. Instead he landed near the Royal Devon and Exeter Hospital and left the injured men in the hands of the NHS after the Navy doctor had explained what had happened.

The two were put on trolleys – still in their flying gear - and left in a corridor so Hughes telephoned Yeovilton to ask if they could send a car as the junior foreign doctor did not seem to understand what was wrong with them.

They were both taken to Lee-on-Solent Naval Hospital where X-rays revealed spinal vertebrae compressions. Hughes took three months to heal before going back to 766 Squadron to complete his course. He eventually reached the rank of lieutenant commander.

McKechnie took longer to recover but went on to have a long career in Navy aviation. In 1967 he piloted one of the Sea Vixens that dropped napalm on the Torrey Canyon which had struck on Seven Stones reef and was leaking crude oil.

He later earned a DSM from the Turkish government for a ship-to-ship transfer by Wasp helicopter in darkness and stormy seas of 72 men of the Turkish Navy who had been rescued after a friendly fire incident during the Cyprus War in 1974. Captain Ian McKechnie, who later became the Queen's harbourmaster on the Clyde, died at the age of 60.

His Sea Vixen was recovered by the Navy soon after the 1966 Dartmoor crash. In 1993 I found a panel at the site with XJ522 painted on the inside.

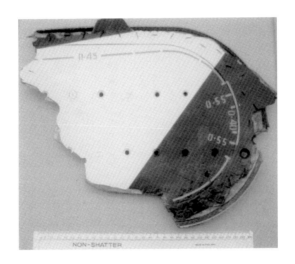

A panel from the Sea Vixen, shown front and back
with the serial number clearly shown on the back

Abbreviations

RAF Ranks

AC	– Aircraftman
Lac	– Leading Aircraftman
AO	– Air Observer
AE	– Air Engineer
Wop/Ag	– Wireless Operator/Air Gunner
Sgt	– Sergeant
F/Sgt	– Flight Sergeant
P/O	– Pilot Officer
F/O	– Flight Officer
W/O	– Warrant Officer
F/Lt	– Flight Lieutenant
S/Ldr	– Squadron Leader
F/Cdr	– Flight Commander
W/Cdr	– Wing Commander

US Airforce Crew

1Lt	– First Lieutenant
2Lt	– Second Lieutenant
Capt	– Captain
Col	– Colonel
Cpl	– Corporal
F/O	– Flight Officer
Gen	– General
Lt Col	– Lieutenant Colonel
Lt Gen	– Lieutenant General
Maj	– Major
Maj Gen	– Major General
M/Sgt	– Master Sergeant
Pfc	– Private First Class
Pvt	– Private
S/Sgt	– Staff Sergeant
WO	– Warrant Officer
W/Cdr	– Wing Commander

US Navy Aircrew

Amm — Aviation Machinists Mate
Aom — Aviation Ordnance Man
Arm — Aviation Radioman
Ens — Ensign

German Aircrew	RAF Equivalent
Feldwebel	Sergeant
Flieger	Aircraftman Second Class
Hauptmann	Flight Lieutenant
Leutnant	Pilot Officer
Gefreiter	Aircraftman First Class
Oberfeldwebel	Flight Sergeant
Obergerfreter	Leading Aircraftman
Oberleutnant	Flying Officer
Unteroffizier	Corporal

General Abbreviations

AA — Anti Aircraft
AI — Airborne Interception
AIU — Accident Investigation Unit
ASB — Anti-Submarine Bomb
Bandit — Enemy Aircraft
BG — Bomber Group
FG — Fighter Group
FS — Fighter Squadron
Flak — German anti-Aircraft Fire
HCU — Heavy Conversion Unit
MU — Maintenance Unit
RA — Royal Artillery
RAF — Royal Air Force
RAFVR — Royal Air Force Volunteer Reserve
RCAF — Royal Canadian Air Force
RAAF — Royal Australian Air Force
RNZAF — Royal New Zealand Air Force
Rho — Rhodesia
PRU — Photo Reconnaissance Unit
Pol — Poland

USN	– United States Navy
USAF	– United States Army Air Force
U/S	– Unserviceable
OCU	– Operational Conversion Unit
OTU	– Operational Training Unit
Sqd	– Squadron
SA	– South Africa
SOC	– Struck off Charge

German Aircraft

Do	– Dornier
Fw	– Focke Wulf
He	– Heinkel
Ju	– Junkers
Me	– Messerschmitt

German Units

F	– Fernaufklarungs	– Long Range Reconnaissance
JG	– Jagdgeschwader	– Fighter Group
LG	– Lehrgeshwader	– Tactical Development Unit Operating with Airborne Forces
KG	– Kampfgruppe	– Bomber Squadron

Roll of Honour

18-01-40	P/O	B. Stevens	RAF
	Sgt	F. Smith	RAF
	Sgt	L. Chenery	RAF
	Ac2	L. Wakely	RAF
	Ac2	W. Heron	RAF

16.05.40	P/O	M.L. Patton-Bethune	RAFVR
	Sgt	K. Stokes	RAFVR
	Lac	H. Morton	RAF
	Ac2	C. Crowcroft	RAF

| 20.11.40 | Sgt | R.T. Thomas | RAFVR |

| 29.12.40 | P/O | D.M. Vine | RAFVR |
| | P/O | W.O.L. Smith | RAF |

21.03.41	P/O	The Hon. R.D. Wilson	RAFVR
	Sgt	R. Ellis	RAFVR (SA)
	Sgt	R. Brames	RAFVR
	Sgt	C. Lyon	RAFVR

04.04.41	F/Lt	R.P.C. Thompson	RAFVR
	P/Off.	L.R. Evans	RAF
	Sgt	L.R. Eden	RAFVR
	Sgt	A.M. Murray	RAFVR

20.04.41	P/Off.	E. Procyk	RAF (Pol)
	Ac2	K.R. Moore	RAFVR
	Ac1	K. Beevers	RAFVR
	Ac1	K. Robbins	RAFVR

19.05.41	Oberlt zur See G. Hitschfeld		
	Uffz	P. Nowacki	
	Uffz	J. Kasten	(All Lufftwaffe)
	Uffz	H. Knor	

| 09.06.41 | W/Cdr | R.C. Hancock | RAF |

27.09.41	P/O	W.T. Gayzler	RAF (P)
	P/O	W.S. Pfleger	RAF (P)
29.11.41	P/O	K. Wojcik	RAF (P)
18.12.41	Sgt	A. Przesmycki (Ground Crew)	RAF (P)
15.03.42	P/O	A.S.R. MacKenzie	RAF (R)
08.05.42	Sgt	J. Oliver	RNZAF
24.05.42	Sgt	A.P. Paterson	RAFVR
	Sgt	L.M. Smith	RAF
	Sgt	R.L. Mellish	RCAF
	Sgt	C.A. Pankhurst	RAFVR
27.08.42	Sgt	G.E. Robertson	RAFVR
	Sgt	P.E.J. Jenkins	RAF
	Sgt	D.H. Harris	RAFVR
	Sgt	D.R. Simpson	RAFVR
	Sgt	L.H. Nicholson	RAFVR
	Sgt	F.S. Clarke	RAFVR
	Sgt	C.J. Bond	RAFVR
06.10.42	F/O	G.H. Edgett	RCAF
	Sgt	E.H. Bastow	RAFVR
	Sgt	J. Bennie	RAFVR
	Sgt	R.L. Partington	RAFVR
30.10.42	F/O	G.M. Sellar	RAFVR
	Sgt	H.O. Dawe	RAFVR
	Sgt	W.G. Fraser	RAFVR
	P/O	W.A. Cruickshanks	RAFVR
	F/O	V.E. Crowther	RNZAF
	P/O	W.B. Martin	RAFVR
02.11.42	F/O	D.K. Robertson	RCAF

09.11.42	Sgt	S.A. Watkins	RAF
	Sgt	D.F. Small	RAF
12.12.42	P/O	W.M.M. Ciechanowski	RAF (Pol)
18.01.43	Lt	R.R.W. Trafford	RNVR
	AA4	J.W. Tyrrell	RN
15.02.43	F/O	R. Dunsmuir	RAF
18.05.43	L/Bdr	W.G. Longhurst	RA
	Gnr	R.V.S. Massey	RA
	Gnr	R. Brittain	RA
01.06.43	Sgt	J.D. Dixon	RAFVR
07.07.43	F/O	E. Gottowt	RAF (Pol)
21.10.43	F/O	S.J. Shewell	RCAF
03.12.43	Lt	T. Lucas	USNR
	Lt	J. Alexander	USNR
	Amm1c	T. Ray	USN
	Amm2c	R. O'Leary	USNR
	Amm3c	E. Shubert	USNR
	Ens	D. Shea	USNR
	Ens	F. Buckley	USNR
	Arm2c	W. Tgan	USN
	Aom2c	W. Davidson	USN
	Aom2c	J. Laubtnger	USNR
25.12.43	2nd Lt	R.T. Neary	USAF
	T/Sgt	S.R. Renner	USAF
	T/Sgt	S.L. Craig	USAF
	S/Sgt	M.A. Panetti	USAF
	S/Sgt	A.J. Blanchard	USAF

27.12.43	Capt	R.L. Williams	USAF
	2nd Lt	J.W. Hanley	USAF
	1st Lt	M.L. Remling	USAF
	T/Sgt	J.A. Wallace	USAF
	T/Sgt	G.O. Wichner	USAF
	S/Sgt	H.D. MacMillan	USAF
	S/Sgt	E.P. Rush	USAF
28.12.43	Lt	W.W. Parish	USNR
	Ens	D.M. Lyons	USNR
	Ens	R.W. Lovelace	USNR
	Amm2c	A.J. Stork	USNR
	Arm2c	L.M. Davenport	USNR
	Arm3c	J.F. Benson	USNR
	Aom3c	A.J. Roddy Jnr	USNR
	Amm3c	C.A. Reynard	USNR
	Amm3c	D. Nash	USNR
	Amm2c	J. Shaffer	USNR
05.01.44	F/Sgt	J.P. Worthington	RAAF
01.03.44	P/O	F.J. Cooke	RAFVR
	F/Sgt	W.M. Jack	RAFVR
	F/Sgt	A.G. Beeston	RAFVR
	Sgt	J.J. Yeates	RAFVR
28.05.44	F/Sgt	J.D. Pringle	RAFVR
12.09.44	F/O	N.H. McDonald	RCAF
	F/O	S.K. McGuigan	RCAF
	F/O	R.W. Murphy	RAFVR
	Sgt	L.W. Bowd	RAFVR
	Sgt	G.J. Canham	RAFVR
	Sgt	G.F. Bennett	RAFVR
	Sgt	T. Hunter	RAFVR
12.05.45	Lac	A. Mastin	RAF
08.06.45	Sgt	K.T. Bakas (Pol)	
	Ac1	C.P. Heaps	RAF

16.07.45	F/O	R. Sloan	RCAF
	F/Sgt	G.C. Moir	RCAF
13.10.45	2nd Lt	R.H. Mara	USAF
	2nd Lt	F.G. McCutchin	USAF
	T/Sgt	M.J. Kack	USAF
	Lt Col	C.R. Rasmussen	US Army
	Pfc	D.L. Klapps	US Army
	Pfc	R. Flower	US Army
	Pvt	V.E. Whiting	US Army
03.01.47	W/O	A.C. Green	RAFVR
18.06.47	Lt	H.D. Easy	RN
	Capt	P.J. Waddington	Army
23.10.47	P/O	A.R. Graham	RAF
29.02.56	F/Sgt	D. Toogood	RAF

List of Aircraft Types

Airspeed Oxford MkI
Avro Anson MKI
Avro Lancaster MKI
Boeing B17G
Boulton Paul Defiant MkII/MkIII
Boulton Paul Balliol T2
Bristol Beaufighter MKIIF/MkVI MkTT10
Bristol Blenheim MkIV
Breguet 693
Consolidated Liberator B24C/MKIII/PB4-Y
Douglas C-47
De Havilland Mosquito NF30
De Havilland Tiger Moth 82A
De Havilland Sea Vixen FAW1
Fairey Battle MkI
Fairey Fulmar MkI
Fairey Firefly FrI
Gloster Gladiator MKI
Hawker Hurricane MKI/MKIIB
Hawker Typhoon MKIB
Handley Page Hampden MKI
Handley Page Harrow MKII
Handley Page Halifax MKII
Junkers JU88A5
Lockheed Hudson
Messerschmitt Me 109-E7
Percival Proctor
Supermarine Spitfire MKI/MKV/MKIVPR/MKXVI/MKXXI
Short Stirling MKIII
North American Mustang MKI
Westland Lysander MKIII
Westland Whirlwind MKI
Vickers Wellington MKIC/MKIII/MKX

ACKNOWLEDGEMENTS

This book would not have been possible without the help of the following individuals and organisations –

Air Historical Branch RAF
Albert F Simpson Historical Research Center, USA
Australian Department of Defence
Bill Wilkinson
Boulton Paul
British Aerospace, Bristol
Commonwealth War Graves Commission
Deutsches Bundesarchiv
Dunkeswell Museum
Gavin Dolland
General Register Office
Imperial War Museum
Jiří Rajlich
Paul Huddart
Polish Institute and Sikorski Museum
Public Archives of Canada
RAF Memorial Museum, Davidstow Moor, Cornwall
RAF Museum
Royal Canadian Air Force
Shorts Ltd
The National Archive (PRO)
United States Air Force
United States Navy
Westland Aircraft, Yeovil
Wilhelm Ratuszynski

The following individuals helped in many different ways and my thanks go to the late Bernard Stevens, the late Basil Browne, the late Philip Jenkinson and the late Frank Mares DFC for photographs; former Dartmoor Ranger Eddie Haines for his memories; Yanna Garnsworthy for translations; David Keast BEM for encouraging me to put my collection of air crash relics on permanent display and allowing me to do so at the RAF Memorial Museum, Davidstow Moor, which he founded; Fay Lewis for typing and Joshua Croxton for the cover design.

I also thank Graham Amhof for information about the Meadows family and Paul Hambling, archivist of the Museum of Dartmoor Life, Okehampton.

Thanks also to Paul Jennings, who walked many miles with me across Dartmoor in all weathers looking for crash sites.

Finally my thanks go to Paul Rendall, the editor, for permission to use material previously published in the Dartmoor News.

Graham J. Lewis,
Davidstow, 2016

BIBLIOGRAPHY

During my research, I consulted various books, the more relevant are listed below with my grateful thanks to the authors.

Action Stations, Chris Ashworth, Patrick Stephens Ltd

Bomber Command Losses, William R Chorley, Midland Counties Publications

The Mighty Eighth, Jane's, 1985, Roger A Freeman

Lancaster File, Air Britain Publications, JJ Halley

High Ground Wrecks, David J. Smith, Midland Publications

The Handley Page Hampden Crash Log, Nicholas Roberts, Midland Publications

The Blitz, Then and Now, After the Battle

Whirlwind, Victor Bingham, Airlife

Devon Aerodromes, Keith Sanders, Alan Sutton Publishing

Spitfire: The History, Eric B Morgan and Edward Shacklady, Key Publishing Ltd

The Stirling Story, Michael JF Bowyer, Crecy Publishing

Lockheed Hudson in World War II, Andrew Hendrie, The Crowood Press Ltd

They Shall Not Grow Old, Commonwealth Airtraining Plan Museum

De Havilland Twin-Boom Fighters: Vampire, Venom, Sea Vixen, Barry Jones, Crowood Aviation Series

The B17 Flying Fortress Story, Roger A Freeman, Arms and Armour

B24 Liberator at War, Roger Freeman, Ian Allan Publishing

Other titles to follow by the author.

Eagles on Lundy

'Aircraft Down' in Devon, volume 1

P.O.W. 507

Manley Bridge Memorial